D0422295

EAGLE VALLEY LIBRARY DISTRICT
1 06 0004944480

READING WITH THE STARS

READING WITH THE STARS

A CELEBRATION OF BOOKS AND LIBRARIES

LEONARD KNIFFEL

WITH

BARACK OBAMA * JULIE ANDREWS * BILL GATES * DAVID MAMET
LAURA BUSH * KEN BURNS * KAREEM ABDUL-JABBAR
COKIE ROBERTS * RON REAGAN * GARRISON KEILLOR * RALPH NADER
JAMIE LEE CURTIS * AL GORE * OPRAH WINFREY

SKYHORSE PUBLISHING

AMERICAN LIBRARY ASSOCIATION
CHICAGO 2011

Reprinted by permission of the authors:
"Archiving America," by Ken Burns
"My Alma Mater," by David Mamet
"A Renaissance in Washington," by Ralph Nader

ALA Editions ISBN: 978-0-8389-3598-9
Skyhorse ISBN: 978-1-61608-277-2

Library of Congress Cataloging-in-Publication Data
Kniffel, Leonard, 1947–
Reading with the stars : why they love libraries / by Leonard Kniffel with Barack Obama, Julie Andrews, Bill Gates, David Mamet, Laura Bush, Ken Burns, Kareem Abdul-Jabbar, Cokie Roberts, Ron Reagan, Garrison Keillor, Ralph Nader, Jamie Lee Curtis, Al Gore, Oprah Winfrey.
pages cm
Includes bibliographical references.
ISBN 978-0-8389-3598-9 (alk. paper)
1. Celebrities—Books and reading—United States. 2. Celebrities—United States—Attitudes. 3. Libraries—United States—Public opinion. 4. Public opinion—United States. 5. Celebrities—United States—Interviews. 6. Library users—United States—Interviews. I. Title.
Z1039.C45K58 2011
027—dc22 2010051954

Book design in Deibi and Charis SIL by Karen Sheets de Gracia.
First edition, first printing 2011.
Printed in China.

CONTENTS

INTRODUCTION

Celebrities have been loving libraries for a very long time, posing for the American Library Association's ubiquitous READ posters, writing testimonials, and giving impassioned speeches about their childhood experiences in that most American of American institutions, the public library.

I remember my first close encounter with a movie star. It was in 1991 and I was a brand new associate editor at *American Libraries*. Oscar winner Glenn Close was in Chicago for the world premiere of her latest film, *Sarah, Plain and Tall*, during the ALA Annual Conference. I snapped photos and buzzed around the periphery of the crowd that surrounded her in the Hilton Hotel as she chatted with the ALA president and other bigwigs. Someone from the ALA staff asked me if I'd like to meet Close, up close. I deferred, thinking to myself, "What in the world would I say to a movie star?"

It took me almost 10 years to get over that attitude and to understand that if movie stars and business moguls, sports stars and stars of the political stage, wanted to volunteer their time to make public service announcements, pose for READ posters, or deliver keynote addresses for ALA, it had little to do with me and much to do with what I represented: the libraries of the United States of America.

There is much to love about celebrities who use their notoriety to promote reading. Of course they want to sell their books, but it's more than that. Looking back on the first decade of the 21st century, it is validating to realize that celebrities—from movie stars to presidents—have chosen to invest their valuable time in the cause of literacy and lifelong learning.

Over the past 10 years, many celebrities have spoken out in support of reading and many agreed to interviews with *American Libraries*. Some gave generously of their time and were gracious and warm; others were more officious and distant. But all were sincere in their willingness to speak out for libraries and the important role they play in the vitality of our nation's educational and cultural future. Now, more than ever, we need their voices, on the record and echoing to all who doubt.

Vartan Gregorian, the great champion of libraries and president of Carnegie Corporation of New York, said at the 2009 I Love My Librarian awards ceremony at the New York Times that librarians must never underestimate their power, the power to offer the rich and famous of today something no one else can: immortality. If in a hundred years, anyone remembers the celebrities in this volume, it will be because librarians preserved the record of their lives, their contribution, and their art. ★

BARACK OBAMA

44th president of the United States of America

1

BOUND TO THE WORD

"Our prosperity as a nation is directly correlated to our literacy."

Barack Obama was a U.S. senator from Illinois when he keynoted the American Library Association's annual conference in Chicago in 2005. He had already exploded onto the American political stage with a stirring speech at the Democratic National Convention the year before and was enjoying growing popularity as an idealist and a unifier. I wish I could say I knew the minute I met him that he had "President of the United States" written all over him. Charismatic and articulate as he was, I might have, had I the confidence that my country was ready to elect an African-American man to that exalted post.

I showed up in the Green Room at McCormick Place convention center and strolled up to him, introduced myself, and shoved a tape recorder in his face. He smiled and said he'd be happy to talk to me. He listened to my questions and pondered each of them for a moment, folding his arms and resting his chin on one hand.

Photo by Pete Souza, courtesy of the White House.

"Can you share your memories about what libraries meant to you as you were growing up?" I asked.

"I lived overseas for several years in Jakarta, Indonesia, when I was young," he replied, "and having access to books—English-language books in particular—was just a huge prize. So when I came back from Indonesia, the first place I wanted to be was in a library. It just always seemed to be a magical place where, if you wanted to sit there, you could learn about everything in the world."

I asked him to talk more about the effect libraries have had on him. To my surprise, he gave me an answer that virtually ended up crediting a librarian at the New York Public Library for launching his political career.

"People always mention libraries in terms of just being sources for reading material or research. But I probably would not be in Chicago were it not for the Manhattan public library, because I was looking for an organizing job and was having great trouble finding a job as a community organizer in New York. The Mid-Manhattan Library had these books of lists of organizations, and the librarian helped me find these lists of organizations, and I wrote to every organization. One of them wound up being an organization in Chicago that I got a job with."

Asked to tell me something that he was not going to say in his speech at the conference, he said, "You know, I have a soft spot in my heart for librarians." Then he quipped, "Although I'll probably mention this in my speech, I have been known to misbehave in libraries."

"What's your main message to librarians?" I asked.

He tilted his head thoughtfully and replied, "That our prosperity as a nation is directly correlated to our literacy."

It was then time for his speech and I joined the crowd in the auditorium where, along with some 5,000 others who heard him talk that day, I was completely blown away. His talk wasn't some canned puffery with "library" occasionally thrown in for relevance. This speech was anything but boilerplate, and it demonstrated an understanding of the sacred mission of the profession. It earned Obama a standing ovation.

The next day, I got on the phone with Obama's people and asked if I could adapt the speech into a cover story for *American Libraries*. Calling librarians guardians of truth and knowledge as well as champions of privacy, literacy, independent thinking, and most of all reading, here are the president's own words, as they appeared in the August 2005 issue.

IF YOU OPEN UP SCRIPTURE, the Gospel according to John, it starts: "In the beginning was the Word." Although this has a very particular meaning in Scripture, more broadly what it speaks to is the critical importance of language, of writing, of reading, of communication, of books as a means of transmitting culture and binding us together as a people.

More than a building that houses books and data, the library represents a window to a larger world, the place where we've always come to discover big ideas and profound concepts that help move the American story forward and the human story forward. That's the reason why, since ancient antiquity, whenever those who seek power would want to control the human spirit, they have gone after libraries and books. Whether it's the ransacking of the great library at Alexandria, controlling information during the Middle Ages, book burnings, or the imprisonment of writers in former communist bloc countries, the idea has been that if we can control the word, if we can control what people hear and what they read and what they comprehend, then we can control and imprison them, or at least imprison their minds.

That's worth pondering at a time when truth and science are constantly being challenged by political agendas and ideologies, at a time when language is used not to illuminate but, rather, to obfuscate, at a time when there are those who would disallow the teaching of evolution in our schools, where fake science is used to beat back attempts to curb global warming or fund life-saving research.

At a time when book banning is back in vogue, libraries remind us that truth isn't about who yells the loudest, but who has the right information.

We are a religious people, Americans are, as am I. But one of the innovations, the genius of America, is recognizing that our faith is not in contradiction with fact and that our liberty depends upon our ability to access the truth.

That's what libraries are about. At the moment that we persuade a child, any child, to cross that threshold, that magic threshold into a library, we change their lives forever, for the better. It's an enormous force for good.

I remember at different junctures in my life feeling lost, feeling adrift, and feeling that somehow walking into a library and seeing those books, seeing human knowledge collected in that fashion, accessible, ready for me, would always lift my spirits. So I'm grateful to be able to acknowledge the importance of librarians and the work that you do. I want to work with you to ensure that libraries continue to be sanctuaries of learning, where we are free to read and consider what we please without the fear

At a time when book banning is back in vogue, libraries remind us that truth isn't about who yells the loudest, but who has the right information. — BARACK OBAMA

that Big Brother may be peering over our shoulders to find out what we're up to.

Some of you may have heard that I gave a speech last summer at the Democratic convention. [Cheering erupted at this point.] It made some news here and there. For some reason, one of the lines people seem to remember has to do with librarians, when I said, "We don't like federal agents poking around our libraries in the red states, or the blue states for that matter."

What some people may not remember is that for years, librarians have been on the front lines of this fight for our privacy and our freedom. There have always been dark times in our history where America has strayed from our best ideas. The question has always been: Who will be there to stand up against those forces? One of the groups that has consistently stood up has been librarians. When political groups tried to censor great works of literature, you were the ones who put *Huckleberry Finn* and *The Catcher in the Rye* back on the shelves, making sure that our access to free thought and free information was protected. Ever since we've had to worry about our own government looking over our shoulders in that library, you've been there to stand up and speak out on our privacy issues. You're full-time defenders of the most fundamental liberty that we possess. For that, you deserve our gratitude.

But you also deserve our protection. That's why I've been working with Republicans and Democrats to make sure that we have a Patriot Act that helps us track down terrorists without trampling on our civil liberties. This is an issue that Washington always tries to make into an either-or proposition. Either we protect our people from terror or we protect our most cherished principles. But I don't believe in either-or. I believe in both ends. I think we can do both. I think when we pose the choice as either-or, it is asking too little of us and it assumes too little about America. I believe we can harness new technologies and a new toughness to find terrorists before they strike, while still protecting the very freedoms we're fighting for in the first place.

I know that some librarians have been subject to FBI or other law enforcement orders asking for reading records. I hope we can pass a provision just like the one that the House of Representatives passed overwhelmingly that would require federal agents to get these kinds of search warrants from a real judge in a real court just like everyone else does.

In the Senate, the bipartisan bill that we're working on, known as the SAFE Act, will prevent the federal government from freely rifling through e-mails and library records without obtaining such a warrant. Giving law enforcement the tools they need to investigate suspicious activity is one thing, but doing it without the approval of our judicial system seriously jeopardizes the rights of all Americans and the ideals Americans stand for. We're not going to stand for it. We need to roll that provision back.

In addition to the line about federal agents poking around in our libraries, there was another line in my speech that got a lot of attention, and it's a line that I'd like to amplify this afternoon. At one point in the speech, I mentioned that the people I've met all across Illinois know that government can't solve all their problems. And I mentioned that if you go into the inner city of Chicago, parents will tell you that parents have to parent. Children can't achieve unless they raise their expectations and turn off the television sets and eradicate the slander that says a black youth with a book is acting white.

To some, that was perceived as speaking solely to the black community. I'm here to suggest that I was speaking to a basic principle, a worry, a challenge, a concern that applies to all of America. Because I believe that if we want to give our children the best possible chance in life, if we want to open the doors of opportunity while they're young and teach them the skills they'll need to succeed later on, then one of our greater responsibilities as citizens, as educators, and as parents is to ensure that every American child can read and read well. That's because literacy is the most basic currency of the knowledge economy that we're living in today.

Only a few generations ago it was possible to enter into the workforce with a positive attitude, a strong back, willing to work. And it didn't matter if you were a high school dropout, you could go into that factory or work on a farm and still hope to find a job that would allow you to pay the bills and raise a family.

That economy is long gone. And it's not coming back. As revolutions in technology and communications began breaking down barriers between countries and connecting people all over the world, new jobs and industries that require more skill and knowledge have come to dominate the economy.

Whether it's software design or computer engineering or financial analysis, corporations can locate these jobs anywhere in the world, anywhere that there's an internet connection. As countries like China and India continue to modernize their economies and educate their children longer and better, the competition American workers face will grow more intense, the necessary skills more demanding. These new jobs are not simply about working hard, they're about what you know and how fast you can learn what you don't know. They require innovative thinking, detailed comprehension, and superior communication.

But before our children can even walk into an interview for one of these jobs, before they can even fill out an application or earn the required college degree, they have to be able to pick up a book and read it and understand it. Reading is the gateway skill that makes all other learning possible, from complex word problems and the meaning of our history to scientific discovery and technological proficiency. And by the way, it's what's required to make us true citizens.

In a knowledge economy where this kind of skill is necessary for survival, how can we send our children out into the world if they're only reading at a 4th-grade level? How can we do it? I don't know. But we do. Day after day, year after year. Right now, one out of every five adults in the United States cannot read a simple story to a child. During the last 20 years or so, over 10 million Americans reached the 12th grade without having learned to read at a basic level. These literacy problems start well before high school. In 2000, only 32% of all 4th-graders tested as reading-proficient.

The story gets worse when you take race and income into consideration. Children from low-income families score 27 points below the average reading level while students from wealthy families score 15 points above the average. While only one in 12 white 17-year-olds has the ability to pick up the newspaper and understand the science section, for Hispanics, the number drops to one in 50; for African Americans, it's one in 100.

In this new economy, teaching our kids just enough so that they can get through *Dick and Jane* is not going to cut it. Over the next 10 years, the average literacy required for all American occupations is projected to rise by 14%.

It's not enough just to recognize the words on the page anymore. The kind of literacy necessary for the 21st century requires detailed understanding and complex comprehension. And, yet, every year we pass more children through schools or watch as more drop out. These are kids who will pore through the help-wanted section and cross off job after job that requires skills they don't have. Others will have to take that help-wanted section over to somebody sitting next to them and find the courage to ask, "Will you read this for me?"

We have to change our whole mindset as a nation. We're living in the 21st-century knowledge economy; but our schools, our homes, and our culture are still based around 20th-century and in some cases 19th-century expectations.

The government has a critical role to play in this endeavor of upgrading our children's skills. This is not the place for me to lay out a long education-reform agenda; but I can say that it doesn't make sense if we have a school system designed for agrarian America and its transition into the industrial age, where we have schools in Chicago that let high school students out at 1:30 because there's not enough money to keep them there any longer, where teachers continue to be underpaid, where we are not restructuring these schools and financing them sufficiently to make sure that our children are going to be able to compete in this global economy.

There is a lot of work to do on the part of government to make sure that we have a first-class educational system, but government alone is not going to solve the problem. If we are going to start setting high standards and inspirational examples for our children to follow, then all of us have to be engaged.

There is plenty that needs to be done to improve our schools and reform education, but this is not an issue in which we can just look to some experts in Washington to solve the problem. We're going to have to start at home. We're going to have to start with parents. And we're going to have to start in libraries. We know that children who start kindergarten with awareness of language and basic letter sounds become better readers and face fewer challenges in the years ahead. We know the more reading material kids are exposed to at home, the better they score with

READ MORE

Recommended by BARACK OBAMA

- ★ ***The Adventures of Huckleberry Finn,*** by Mark Twain
- ★ ***The Catcher in the Rye,*** by J. D. Salinger
- ★ ***Goodnight Moon,*** by Margaret Wise Brown and Clement Hurd

reading tests throughout their lives. So we have to make investments in family-literacy programs and early-childhood education so that kids aren't left behind and are not already behind the day they arrive at school.

We have to get books into our children's hands early and often. I know this is easier said than done, oftentimes. Parents today still have the toughest job in the world. And no one ever thanks parents for doing it. Not even your kids. Maybe especially your kids, as I'm learning.

Most of you are working longer and harder than ever, juggling job and family responsibilities, trying to be everywhere at once. When you're at home, you might try to get your kids to read, but you're competing with other by-products of the technology revolution, TVs and DVDs and video games, things they have to have in every room of the house. Children 8 to 18 spend three hours a day watching television; they spend 43 minutes a day reading.

Our kids aren't just seeing these temptations at home, they're seeing them everywhere, whether it's their friend's house or the people they see on television or a general culture that glorifies anti-intellectualism. . . . That message trickles down to our kids. It's too easy for children to put down a book and turn their attention elsewhere. And it's too easy for the rest of us to make excuses for it, pretending if we put a baby in front of a DVD that's "educational," then we're doing our jobs. If we let a 12-year-old skip reading as long as he's playing a "wholesome" video game, then we're doing okay. That as long as he's watching PBS at night instead of having a good conversation about a book with his parents, that somehow we're doing our job.

We know that's not what our children need. We know that's not what's best for them. And so as parents, we have to find the time and the energy to step in and help our children love reading. We can read to them, talk to them about what they're reading, and make time for this by turning off the television set ourselves.

Libraries are a critical tool to help parents do this. Knowing the constraints that parents face from a busy schedule and TV culture, we have to think outside the box, to dream big, like we always have in America, about how we're going to get books into the hands of our children.

Right now, children come home from their first doctor's appointment with an extra bottle of formula. They should come home with their first library card or their first copy of *Goodnight Moon.* I have memorized *Goodnight Moon,* by the way: "In the great green room there was a telephone . . ." I love that book.

It should be as easy to get a book as it is to rent a DVD or pick up McDonald's. What if instead of a toy in every Happy Meal there was a book?

Libraries have a special role to play in our knowledge economy. Your institutions have been and should be a place where parents and children come to read together and learn together. We should take our kids there more.

We should make sure our politicians aren't closing libraries down because they had to spend a few extra bucks on tax cuts for folks who don't need them and weren't even asking for them.

Each of you has a role to play. You can keep on getting more children to walk through your doors by building on the ideas

Right now, children come home from their first doctor's appointment with an extra bottle of formula. They should come home with their first library card or their first copy of *Goodnight Moon.* — BARACK OBAMA

that so many of you are already pursuing: book clubs and contests, homework help, and advertising your services throughout the community.

In the years ahead, this is our challenge, and this has to be our responsibility. As a librarian or a parent, every one of you can probably remember the look on a child's face after finishing their first book.

During the campaign last year, I was asked by a reporter from the *Chicago Sun-Times* if she could interview me about the nature of my religious faith. It was an interesting proposition. I sat down with the reporter, who asked me some very pointed questions about the nature of my faith, how it had evolved. Then the reporter asked me a surprising question. She asked me, "Do you believe in heaven? And what's your conception of it?"

I told her, I don't presume to know what lies beyond, but I do know that when I sit down with my 6-year-old and my 3-year-old at night and I'm reading a book to them and then I tuck them in to go to sleep, that's a little piece of heaven that I hang on to.

That was about a year ago, and what's interesting now is watching my 6-soon-to-be-7-year-old reading on her own now. My 4-year-old will still sit in my lap, but my 7-year-old, she lies on the table and on her own. She's got the book in front of her. She's kind of face down, propped up. And I say, "Do you want

READ MORE

Written by BARACK OBAMA

- *Of Thee I Sing: A Letter to My Daughters*
- *The Audacity of Hope: Thoughts on Reclaiming the American Dream*
- *Dreams from My Father: A Story of Race and Inheritance*

me to read to you?" "No, Daddy, I'm all right," she says, and there's a little heartbreak that takes place there.

Yet, when I watch her, I feel such joy because I know that in each of those books she's picking up, her potential will be fulfilled. That's not unique to me. It's true of all of us who are parents. There's nothing we want more than to nurture that sense of wonder in our children. To make all those possibilities and all those opportunities real for our children, to have the ability to answer the question: "What can I be when I grow up?" with the answer "Anything I want. Anything I can dream of."

It's a hope that's old as the American story itself. From the moment the first immigrants arrived on these shores, generations of parents worked hard and sacrificed whatever was necessary so that their children could not just have the same chances they had, but could have the chances they never had. Because while we can never assure that our children will be rich or successful, while we can never be positive that they will do better than their parents, America is about making it possible to give them the chance, to give every child the ability to try. Education is the foundation of this opportunity.

The most basic building block that holds that foundation together is the Word. "In the beginning was the Word."

At the dawn of the 21st century, where knowledge is literally power, where it unlocks the gates of opportunity and success, we all have responsibilities as parents, as librarians, as educators, as politicians, and as citizens to instill in our children a love of reading so that we can give them a chance to fulfill their dreams. That's what all of you do each and every day, and for that, I am grateful. ★

JULIE ANDREWS

actress, singer, children's author

2

MUSIC TO HER EARS

"Words, wisdom, wonder; there is no greater gift we can give our children."

"Let's get to work," Julie Andrews seemed to be saying from the moment she stepped out of a black SUV until the moment the curtain went up on her program at the 2007 American Library Association Annual Conference in Washington, D.C.

Not the attitude one necessarily expects from a movie star who is so famous she cannot appear in public without causing a commotion. Once she had agreed to keynote *American Libraries*' 100th anniversary program, Julie Andrews more or less said, "I'm at your service. What would you like me to do?"

What she did, of course, was nearly cause the crowd to break down the doors to get in, and then she brought down the house with a rousing speech preceded by a video recap of her astonishing singing and acting career on stage, in films, and on television. But Andrews mostly came to the conference to talk about books and her 30-plus years as a children's author and to throw her support behind libraries and the literacy and lifelong learning they represent.

Photo by Mattox Photography for the American Library Association.

Following the speech, the indefatigable Andrews signed a hundred copies of her books, spoke at a luncheon for children's librarians, sat for a photo shoot for the cover of *American Libraries* with a group of rambunctious children, read from *The Great American Mousical* to the same children, and then agreed to be honorary chair of National Library Week 2008 at a press conference at the District of Columbia Public Library, where she called National Library Week "a time to honor the contributions of our nation's libraries and librarians and the degree to which they transform communities."

"Libraries have always been places of opportunity, places where everyone—regardless of age, race, or income—can come together, whether for research, entertainment, self-help, or to find that one special book," she said.

Andrews said she wanted to use her visibility and celebrity "to remind the public about the value of all of our libraries and librarians in each and every community throughout America," adding, "I am deeply honored to help champion that cause."

Along with her daughter and frequent coauthor Emma Walton Hamilton, Andrews read from *Mousical* to the children assembled on the scruffy library floor for the press conference and the photo shoot. Said Hamilton, "We are deeply concerned about the fact that, despite their increased attendance, school libraries were hard hit by funding cuts in the past year. Libraries need the support of the public to influence our decision-makers to provide increased library funding."

"You represent some of the finest and most dedicated librarians in the country," said entertainment icon Andrews at the centennial program. "I so applaud the work that you all do, and the difference that you are making in the lives of children. Our youngsters of tomorrow will face more choices and have to make more decisions in their brave new world than you and I have ever known."

"I've been working in the performing arts for over 50 years, which by *American Libraries* standards puts me at about mid-career!" she quipped. "And though it may seem a little unusual for an 'immigrant' such as myself to speak at an American Library Association event, I have made America my home for the past 45 years, am married to an American, and have five American children and seven American grandchildren, so I have a huge appreciation for this country and the gifts and opportunities it offers people of all nationalities," said the British-born star.

Andrews said that "in certain circles I am perceived as a 'celebrity author,' and I have to admit this really irritates me, as I have been writing children's books professionally for over 35 years now. Actually, if you think about it, my life in the arts has always been about evoking images—either through song or the spoken word. Writing for me is an extension of that voice."

Andrews noted that 10 years before, she and Hamilton began collaborating as authors. To date they have written 20 children's books together. The mother-daughter duo recently began collaborating on a "classroom partnership program," the goal of which, said Andrews, was to help teachers "develop activities that encourage the connection of graded-level reading with theatrical,

A library takes the gifts of reading one step further. In this day of standardized and homogenized education, a library offers individual and personalized learning opportunities second to none. —JULIE ANDREWS

musical, and artistic expression, to provide an opportunity for students to interact directly with us as authors, and to work in partnership with schools and performing arts centers around the country to develop stage adaptations of books from the Julie Andrews Collection."

"I have been enormously fortunate in my professional career as an actress to receive the kind of media attention that has given me the opportunity to become an advocate for literacy, a privilege that I do not take lightly," said Andrews.

"In today's media and electronically driven world, I feel that children run the risk of becoming very isolated. I worry that we are spoon-feeding our young people such a steady diet of manufactured slices of life that all they have to do is receive rather than participate in any way. The joy of reading is that it asks us to *engage,* to use our imaginations and to play an active role in our environment.

"A library takes the gifts of reading one step further. In this day of standardized and homogenized education, a library offers individual and personalized learning opportunities second to none," said Andrews. "Perhaps most importantly, libraries offer a powerful antidote to the isolation of the Web, providing connection, support, and community. Rather than wading in a solitary fashion through the morass of potential misinformation available on the Net, the student who conducts his or her explorations at a library has safe, professional guidance in their search for good books and accurate information." Provoking laughter and applause, she alluded to a recent uproar over *The Higher Power of Lucky*: "I, for one, would far prefer that my children and grandchildren learn the meaning of the word 'scrotum' from a library than from the playground or Web surfing!"

Andrews concluded, "We share a special partnership, working to illuminate young hearts and minds every day. It is an awesome responsibility, but I cannot think of one more rewarding or more worthwhile."

As National Library Week chair, Julie Andrews authored a piece for *American Libraries* titled "Seven Special Days," which began, "Library workers of the world, my hat's off to you!" She went on to say that "as honorary chair of this year's celebration, part of my responsibility is to thank you, the library workers of the world, for all that you do throughout the year.

"As a mother and grandmother, one of my greatest pleasures in life has been watching the children learn and grow. It has never been clearer than now, at a time when our young people are bombarded with so many distractions, that reading and literacy, open inquiry and creativity, are essential to that core American value: the pursuit of happiness.

"Now more than ever children need the skills necessary to make good judgments about the sometimes overwhelming amount of information and entertainment that is available in their lives today. Your profession represents and promotes the kind of independent learning and thinking that equips children

READ MORE

Recommended by JULIE ANDREWS

- ★ ***The Higher Power of Lucky,*** by Susan Patron
- ★ ***Raising Bookworms: Getting Kids Reading for Pleasure and Empowerment,*** by Emma Walton Hamilton
- ★ ***The Secret Garden,*** by Frances Hodgson Burnett
- ★ ***The Secret Island,*** by Enid Blyton
- ★ ***Watership Down,*** by Richard Adams

to take their places in the world as productive and fulfilled adults.

"The world is full of magical places, and the library has always been one of them for me. A library can be that special place for our children. But along with an inviting and safe environment, young readers need the human touch, the guidance and caring of trained professionals, if they are to enjoy the lifetime of learning and literacy we all wish for.

"Thanks to you, library use is up nationwide, continuing a decade-long trend. American libraries are a vital community resource, filling an educational role that is unique in the world, delivering everything from homework help to literacy tutoring.

"I also understand that many libraries, especially in schools, are struggling in the face of funding shortages. I want to do my part to help the public understand what a mistake it is to cut support for libraries and education."

Following National Library Week, Andrews wrote an op-ed piece that appeared in the *Los Angeles Times,* in which she said, "Whenever I have been privileged to visit the Los Angeles Central Library, I have been struck by the words inscribed on its façade: 'Books alone are liberal and free. They give to all who ask. They emancipate all who serve them faithfully.'"

"So I was greatly alarmed to learn that in the face of a very serious city budget shortfall, Mayor Antonio Villaraigosa and the City Council have proposed cuts to our 72 city libraries that will reduce their very lifeblood—those liberating books themselves. They propose to shrink next year's book-buying budget by $2 million—at a time when people need and want a wider variety of books, not fewer of them.

"As an adoptive Angeleno who has called this city home for four decades, I've grown to appreciate Los Angeles's great public library system, which serves the largest population in the nation. But its book funds have been cut so low that today our library system ranks near the bottom of the book-buying list among the nation's 25 largest public library systems. I find it astonishing that our library has only 1.6 books for each resident of Los Angeles—a city that is one of the cultural hubs of this country. San Francisco's library system has 7.3 books per capita; New York's has 6.2.

"It is my sincere hope that our city leaders will revisit their proposal and restore—rather than reduce—funding for our library's books. I can assure you that such an outcome would truly be music to my ears and a blessing for the millions who use and rely on our libraries each day."

But Julie Andrews's support for libraries didn't start with the American Library Association. She filled the enormous convention center auditorium to capacity for her keynote speech April 26, 2006, at the Texas Library Association's annual conference in Houston. She talked about her writing as "a lifelong passion" that began when she was a child performer with a tutor who "allowed me to scribble all I wanted."

Andrews said that at this stage in life she wants to channel whatever media attention her movie-star status offers into advocacy for reading, which is "all about children learning to use their imaginations. Words, wisdom, wonder," she said, "there is no greater gift we can give our children." She talked about how the response of wave after wave of youngsters to her films has made her feel a sense of responsibility to them. Andrews said it was a thrill to have children come up to her and say that one of her books had turned them on to reading.

"Books are an extension of my singing voice," Andrews said, and although that glorious voice was damaged during vocal cord surgery in 1997, she recorded a song four weeks earlier called "The Show Must Go On," available on the website of the Julie Andrews Collection. "It's always been about the words," she added, quoting Gabriel García Márquez: "Words matter; books count."

Thanks to HarperCollins and the persuasive powers of Texas Library Association executive director Patricia Smith, the star of *The Sound of Music* and *Mary Poppins* took time after her keynote speech to talk with me and with *Texas Library Journal* editor Gloria Meraz about her faith in the importance of teaching children the joy of reading.

Asked where her writing inspiration comes from, Andrews said, "It comes from anyplace. Truthfully, once the antennae are kind of up I'm always thinking or looking or feeling. The first book, *Mandy,* happened because we were filming on this wonderful old Georgian estate in Ireland. We actually lived on the property as well as filmed there and were able to discover how people must have lived in the old days. And the cavernous rooms, they were so beautiful—these glorious Georgian windows that looked out over this vast park. And they did, in fact, have a little shell cottage on the grounds, which is the theme of *Mandy.* When I was thinking of what to write for my [stepdaughter] Jenny—she had been raised more in the city than in the country—I thought, well, she doesn't know very much about country life

READ MORE

Written by Julie Andrews

- *Dragon: Hound of Honor* (with Emma Walton Hamilton)
- *The Great American Mousical* (with Emma Walton Hamilton and Tony Walton)
- *Home: A Memoir of My Early Years*
- *Julie Andrews' Collection of Poems, Songs, and Lullabies* (with Emma Walton Hamilton and James McMullan)
- *The Last of the Really Great Whangdoodles*
- *Mandy*

and so maybe that's what I can do to begin to bond with her. And that idea came. And the idea for *The Last of the Really Great Whangdoodles*: I was looking something else up in *Webster's*.

That little mouse in *The Great American Mousical* honestly is a true story. He was running around in our wardrobe, and it was as if a lightbulb came on. I thought, oh my God. Then somebody made a joke about it: he probably came up to see all the big stars up here, and I thought, oh God, of course, they're always down there! What would they know if they were able to think and feel and see? So we had delicious fun writing it.

Andrews's first book, *Mandy,* published in 1971, seems to have tapped into something universal. Girls, especially, are still reading it, and it's never been out of print. I asked her what she thinks that special thing is. "I think it's evocative of many other books," Andrews said. "It was the first book I ever wrote. I mean it's like *The Secret Garden*; its universal theme is how much we all yearn to belong."

I had my own theory. I told her I thought that it's about children without adults, and those kinds of books fascinate children.

"Yes. How do they survive," she agreed. "In my youth, I read an Enid Blyton book called *The Secret Island,* and the children think their parents have been downed in an aircraft and they weren't seemingly coming back, and they're very, very unhappy, and they removed themselves to an island on a river or a lake."

The Great American Mousical, coauthored with Hamilton and illustrated by former husband Tony Walton, is a delightful introduction for children to the theater—its language, conventions, and personalities. Complimented on *Mousical* and its wonderful use of language and such magical language, Andrews said, "Oh thank you. You couldn't have said anything lovelier." And there it was, the lilting British accent, the voice that people love.

Andrews also talked about the glossary in the back of *Mousical.*" The fun was to bring it down to size for children, the

Great White Way. I love the idea of coming down from a star and coming down and then down and then down and then down into the basement, and by that time you've reduced everything."

Asked if *Mousical* was easier and faster to write because of the familiar topic, Andrews laughed. "Well it was faster than some because, first of all, it was ridiculous fun. I mean the idea of that diva and when she says, 'What's to discuss? I'm the star.' You know, I've seldom heard anybody talk like that. But it was such fun to imagine that she was serious. And I love it when she says, 'I'd so love you to have seen my performance. It was completely my evening you know.' It's just what all the ego-driven people might say, and it was terrific fun. We really did tap into people that we might know. I mean, the idea of all these little mice running around with *The King and I* headdresses on, in 'The March of the Siamese Children,' things like that. You know, imagination can create a silly image. We were having a great time."

Asked if her varied career in so many different media helped her find that sense of wonder and the magic, Andrews replied, "It comes from those early days with my father and my wonderful tutor. Particularly my dad. We used to go for long walks together. And I think also when I was married to Tony Walton, there were days—because he's such a fine artist—when he'd point something out and the world would shift just that little bit. I remember we were lying on the grass once and I was

In my youth, living in Walton-on-Thames . . . the library was "the big place" . . . where you went and then suddenly you could access something magical. —JULIE ANDREWS

just looking up at the sun and all that kind of thing. He said, 'My God, look at the leaves on that tree above us. It's like lace up there.' And I hadn't seen the leaves. I'd seen some of the general picture, but suddenly it all pulled in and I saw what he saw and I thought, my God, you can view the world differently if you pay attention.

"I want to do a book one day about—although it's been done—a tree. I've long wanted to write it (it's just finding the time) because a tree is actually a miracle that's every 20 yards down the street under children's noses, but I don't think they ever look or say, 'Wow, how does it feed itself? What lives in it? How does it draw up? And what's the sap doing? And all of that.' So if I could make that into a little story, that's what I'm talking about, a sense of wonder."

I mentioned the beautiful song from *Flower Drum Song* called "A Hundred Million . . ." and she finished my sentence, "'Miracles Are Happening Every Day.' Yes, yes. And I do think that's true. If you can take the time to look. It took me a while to learn that, though some children know it instinctively and they do have wonder when they are kids. But the trouble is, as we grow older, we lose it."

Asked what role libraries have played in her life or are playing now, Andrews said, "Well not so much now, but in my youth, living in Walton-on-Thames in England, it was just a little country village, and the library was 'the big place.' It looked like just an ordinary sort of old-looking schoolhouse, but it was a place where you went and then suddenly you could access something magical. And one couldn't afford all of the books one wanted in those days.

"It's only something that I realized as I began to write and to travel and meet people, because you suddenly see the passion that's out there, and it's lovely. And I do think, where would kids be if it weren't for you and for the good pediatricians, and for the good parents? I passionately believe in sitting a child on your lap and tracing the lines of the book with your finger, and they can read before they know they can, if you bother enough. I did it with my kids, and they're doing it with their kids now."

I wanted her to talk about her legacy, about what she will leave behind, so I mentioned that the Library of Congress maintains the National Film Registry. "They're a great organization, phenomenal," she opined. "They've asked me to donate all my papers there actually, which I'm thrilled about."

I told her that Librarian of Congress James Billington had called for more nominations to the National Film Registry, and one of her films, *The Sound of Music*, had already been added. Then I asked which of her films she would add next, were she choosing. Andrews said that was "probably a foregone conclusion, if it's a National Film Registry for children everywhere" meaning *Mary Poppins* would undoubtedly be the second choice. But I told her the films are selected because they are culturally, historically, or esthetically significant. They're placed on this film registry as an effort to permanently preserve and make accessible these films to the American people.

"Oh, so it's not just for children. I see. Well, then that's different. Oh my. Well I'd really have to think about that. There are some films that my husband [Blake Edwards] made, of course. *Days of Wine and Roses* is a very important film about alcoholism.

"But what about *your* films?" I pressed.

"There was a film—and you're going to think I'm crazy—that he and I made together and it's not what you'd expect me to say. It is called *S.O.B.* It is truly a slice, a real cut at Hollywood. But it has become a cult film, and I think it's a marvelous piece of work. I really do. I think it's riotously funny and silly and everybody remembers, of course, that I bared my breasts, but it was all done for a reason: that aren't we all silly, and what Hollywood is up to and media hype and all that kind of thing. So that one maybe.

And maybe *The Americanization of Emily* because of the point that it makes about making heroes of our dead, and our anthem, therefore propagating war."

"Not so much antiwar, but antiheroization?"

"Exactly. Glamorizing it being very wrong. And, oh gosh, you could go on and on. Those two will do. Blake made a wonderful cowboy movie called *The Wild Rovers,* and it's a little-known film of his. But he deliberately tried to do something that I think is rather interesting. He wanted the audience to root for the wrong guys. He wanted to see if the bad guys could be so damned attractive that you wanted them to survive and that the good guys were so unbelievably mean and mean-spirited. They're not good but really have their own hang-ups and their demons. And I think he succeeded. I watched Blake write it. Every voice in it is part of him—the cowboy that says, 'Hey, I want it now. I don't want to wait till I'm 98 years old and still struggling.' It's a very good movie. It was cut to ribbons, but that's another story."

Asked if there were other books that influenced her as a child, Andrews named *The Little Grey Men*, which she liked so much she republished it in the Julie Andrews Collection. "I know I harp on my father a great deal," she said, "but he bought that for me when I was about 10 years old, and it hit me the way *Watership Down* might hit you if you were reading that today. It was a beautiful nature study. But, again, I really got the idea of bringing things down to size for children and yet teaching them so much. Through that little book I really became aware of every aspect of nature, and it influenced me a great deal. It's no accident that that book takes in the four seasons and that my best book, *Mandy,* takes in the four seasons too. It just seemed like a wonderful way to signify the passage of time and all that. And you really do see nature in all its glory. It's a wonderful little book. If you love reading children's books, it's really great. It hadn't been published here for years and years and years. It's still in publication in England and I've had the rights to it for years. I'd love to see it done as an animated film.

"I suppose partially because of the success of the early movies and things like that, I began to realize, that children do look up to you in some way, and there is a responsibility for how you behave with them. I know that it's important to make them feel very valuable, not to talk down to them. And I try not to when we write."

Gloria Meraz said, "It's so wonderful the way you talk about your efforts to promote literacy because it's an important message for librarians to hear. So often they feel like the unsung heroes. When someone of your stature is talking about how important literacy is and what they do, it elevates them."

"Try to imagine how daunting it is to be on a panel with someone like David [McCullough], all these wonderful authors at the National Book Festival," said Andrews. "And they're asking you to get up and read from your work. I was on a panel with people who were reading excerpts from their books, and [McCullough] was doing it and several other people were, and I was last. And I read a little, tiny bit from *Little Bo,* one of my early, early books, and I go, what am I doing up here? But it's all valuable, I suppose, a different take on things. They were very tactful with me."

Asked for her views on technology and social changes that children are facing, she said, "I see it with my grandchildren—some of my grandchildren, not all of them. The only hope is that you can engage them enough. All it takes is one book. I mean literally one book will do it. And our one daughter reads all the time and then reads again and again. I mean she loves books, I mean really adores them. The other one has a real problem reading, and I keep looking for that one thing, because she just walks away from it and I cannot make it happen for her. She really does have a perception problem, I think. As I say, it takes one book. And I see my little grandson, who is 8, is a whiz at all these computer games, but that's it. And he's a genius at it, and I'm told that they can be very stimulating to children; they can inspire all kinds of things. Not that I knock them, but all he does is zap people and cream people and kill people, you know, and he's having a fine old time and in his head I don't know where he's at. But I keep looking for the one moment that I can say, here, how about that one, you know? That's all it takes, and I guess you just wait and watch and hope that you can be there at the moment that they can get turned on. It's a thrill to hear children come up to me and say *Mandy* was my first book or *Whangdoodle* was my first book and it made me want to read more. Because that's how I discovered it, you know."

Asked, "What's still on your life list?" Andrews said, "Oh, a hundred more books. I hope I live long enough to do them. I have to say that this has surprised me as much as it might surprise anybody else. It's something that's ongoing and I'm discovering as I go. I guess I always thought that as I got older maybe I'd have the time to write something but it never occurred to me that it would be such a joy to work with my daughter or that she'd be the one who's the whiz at it. Of course she's very tapped into the media side of it. But she's far smarter than I am, she writes better than I do. But it's such a joy. It's something that I'm just learning as I go and I'm having a wonderful time doing it because, now that I'm not singing, it is an extension of the voice, and when she pointed that out to me I thought, wow, yeah it can be."

Asked if she really enjoys the process of writing, Andrews said, "The actual process is tough, it's like learning a role where you never think you're going to be able to conquer it when you start and it just takes enough focus and narrowing and getting enthusiastic and not losing it and so on. But the other thing I do love is that I'm never lonely when I'm writing, because you live with the characters that are so alive in your mind, and you really see them and know them and get to be friends with them. So in a way I do hate the process of writing. It's never good enough, but you aim for something and you hope it comes somewhat close. But it is a pleasure once you have written it."

"We all often wonder how being a performer changed your life, but how did writing change your performing, if it did?" I asked.

"That's a good question. The immediate answer off the top of my head is that I don't think it did. I think if something changed my life it would be the idea that scenes and characters are rather important, and my husband stresses that all the time. He says you can have the flimsiest story but if your characters are strong enough you've got something going for you." ★

BILL GATES

philanthropist, founder of Microsoft

3

TAKE ME TO YOUR READER

"Anybody who can get to a library can get to the internet."

Imagine that you're the richest man in the world. Now imagine all the vain and frivolous ways you could spend your money. Do any of them involve riding around rural Alabama in a bookmobile?

"There are two important things about spending this day with librarians," said Microsoft founder Bill Gates in 1998 during a whirlwind tour of Alabama one year into his library philanthropy. "One is for me to learn from them how the process is going and what we can do to help out more and to see the physical environment." The other "is to celebrate the great work they've done in making this happen. Our grant is an impetus, it's a catalyst, but these librarians hold their communities together and get them enthused about this, about having it be very high-visibility."

With only one state connectivity project under way, the enormity of Gates's gift was not clear to anyone at the time. But it

Photo by Jason Alden for Bloomberg, courtesy of Getty Images.

was apparent that when the wealthiest man in the world, at age 43, announced that he intended to begin showering America's libraries with computers and high-speed internet connections, stars were indeed falling on Alabama.

I followed Bill Gates and his wife, Melinda, around Alabama's so-called Black Belt as the couple made their way through the countryside in a bookmobile dubbed Take Me to Your Reader.

Amid cameras and reporters, they visited the public libraries in Montgomery, Selma, and Demopolis that were to be among the first beneficiaries of their foundation's grand plan for closing the information divide by making computers available at libraries in poor communities, starting with the poorest state in the union.

When I interviewed him during that trip, what I remember most is how intense he was and the way he rocked in his chair—the way really smart little kids do when they cannot express a thought fast enough.

I asked Gates what he thought about the future of the book. "We're very, very clear that the role these computers play in no way diminishes what libraries should be doing with books, in terms of growing their collections and keeping them up-to-date." Presciently, he noted that "fifteen years from now, you might be able to read [books] off of a screen, but that doesn't really change anything. The authors are still doing the same thing and want to be compensated for the work they are doing, and people still want a place to go and find those things and ask questions about them, the same way that the newspaper still has reporters who fill the same central role. Even if some day you read it off the screen, the same would be true of written material."

The foundation's library program started with a pilot project in 1996, continued in 1997 with the establishment of the Gates Library Foundation (as it was then called), which invested nearly $180 million in library computerization over five years. At that point, the Bill and Melinda Gates Foundation began a series of sustainability grants and expanded its global reach.

In a second interview with *American Libraries* in 2003, Gates, then Microsoft chairman, said the five-year run of the Bill and Melinda Gates Foundation's library computerization project is the stuff that makes him love his job, and it's people and their stories that keep him going.

This latter-day Andrew Carnegie explained by telephone from Microsoft headquarters in Washington State why he did it and what he hopes it will mean to communities far into the future. I told him that the feedback from my follow-up trip to Alabama had been very positive and asked how the outcome looked to him.

"I'm glad to hear that," he said. "You know, in a lot of philanthropy, things don't go very well. And yet everything we see suggests that for this one the librarians really pitched in and drove this thing to make a big impact, in terms of how people view the library and really reaching out to a lot more people."

I asked him if he felt there were barriers that had to be overcome.

"When we first got into it, we thought there might be a lot of issues: Would the librarians be enthusiastic? Would we be able to train them? Would the constituents show up? Would the constituents use it for things that are basically constructive?" It was telling, he said, that Microsoft executive Patty Stonesifer was so impressed by the library program that when she retired from the company she wanted nothing more than to become president of the foundation.

"There were some amazing things about these rural libraries and the connectivity. We started out where there was the most need, that is, where there were households that didn't have PCs. Therefore, for the kids to get to this tool whenever they wanted to, the library was the only institution that was going to provide that. We also ended up being in states where the connectivity problems were particularly tough, primarily in the rural areas. That took a lot of creativity. It took state-level involvement.

"A lot of the states stepped up very quickly to help with the connectivity costs. I remember Louisiana was particularly good in being one of the first, and then some of the others came along. The energy of the kids that we got into the training effort was really quite phenomenal. They had to travel to all sorts of unusual places for training. And then the librarians really were the ones who made it come together, being enthused about the training and providing space in their libraries and getting the word out. And then, of course, the librarians have had the ongoing challenge of the connectivity costs. We funded training and the initial hardware grants, and Microsoft provided some of the software that people used, but the connectivity piece is ongoing. The federal e-rate discount program helped some, but what's always going to be a challenge is that the local constituency will have to see the additional cost of this connectivity as something that they really want to make sure gets funded for these libraries.

"Most of the concerns we had turned out to not be an issue—the way people use the machines, the involvement of the librarians. There's been the controversy that you would expect over whether filtering software gets put on the machines or not, and we stayed out of that. We don't require any filtering software, nor do we have any issues about whatever choices librarians make about the various filtering options that are out there," Gates said.

The American Library Association had been under fire from the religious right for supporting unfiltered internet access for children in public libraries. I asked Gates what he thought of the criticism that bringing the internet into the library brings pornography to children.

"Fortunately, in the last three or four years, the interest in some kind of filtering by parents has been high enough that many companies, including Microsoft, AOL, and others, have gotten more sophisticated about making filtering capabilities available. Now, those solutions are never perfect. That is, they'll sometimes—and it'll often get publicity—filter out a page like a breast cancer page that maybe should be available, and they'll sometimes filter in something that shouldn't be available. They're not perfect, but they're awfully good. These computers can keep logs of what's been blocked out. Most of the software now allows the librarian, who's got an admin privilege to look at a page and allow it to pass through, to know what's being filtered or even if a patron is there and they're saying, 'Hey, I'm getting this block.' The librarian can walk up, and with most software packages, give the admin password and see what it is and then decide whether to let it pass through or not. In a few cases, you'd have to call the librarian over to make that work. So I feel good that, unlike five years ago, if people do choose to use the software, there's some relatively inexpensive and relatively high-quality stuff that strikes a pretty good balance on these issues.

"To be frank, if you really wanted ultimate precision, you'd almost want different filtering for different ages. And that gets fairly complicated. I actually think librarians put more energy into this than some of the schools have. At least in the case of the library, you have people walking by that screen on a fairly regular basis, and I don't think if I was a kid I'd go to the library and . . . . Anyway, I think it's kind of a public thing, and the librarian

READ MORE

Recommended by BILL GATES

- ★ ***The Catcher in the Rye,*** by J. D. Salinger
- ★ ***Holes,*** by Louis Sachar
- ★ ***A Separate Peace,*** by John Knowles

has the right to walk by and see what you're doing at any point, so the data we have suggest that of all the computer access going on, the amount of any of this kind of activity is very, very small. With or without the filtering, you know, it's not the venue where this is going on."

I asked Gates what link he saw between the foundation's library activities and its health-care initiatives.

"As we looked at what patrons were doing with the library computers, a few things really jumped out. Certainly staying in touch with relatives that are far away and looking for jobs are two big things that we expected. Another that jumped out was that when a friend or family member would have a health issue, they'd be going online to seek information about the disease and what new things might be available in terms of treatment. That was a major activity, and one they're very gratified to be able to get lots of information on.

"The foundation's role in health has been particularly focused on the health needs of poor countries and things like the AIDS epidemic, malaria, tuberculosis. We're partly engaged in trying to raise the awareness of people in this country about the fact that health conditions for most of the people on the planet are still very bad and that research dollars and development dol-

The fact that people who stay in rural areas can stay in touch with people and get at information sources they wouldn't otherwise have, that's just a fantastic thing. The whole role of the library in these rural communities is amazing. It's an organization point for a lot of community activities. — BILL GATES

lars aren't going in to help people with problems that hold them back from achieving a reasonable livelihood. These things don't appear in the news very much because they're constant problems. You just won't see a headline. Yet little of the money in health goes toward these poor countries, even though with infant mortality, the equivalent of five major plane crashes are taking place every day, and the AIDS epidemic is exploding.

"I think these computers have been a great tool to empower people to learn about these things. Certainly our foundation puts up a lot of material and links to various sites. I'm an avid user of the internet to stay up on research work and what's going on in the various conferences. Access to information is just night and day versus five years ago. Because these health issues really appeal to people's humanitarian instincts, hopefully information access will lead to more involvement."

Gates had been quoted as saying that before he died he planned to give away 95% of his wealth. I asked what motivated him and what he saw as the future of libraries.

"Well, hopefully I have a lot of time to think about how this money should go back to society in the best way possible," he laughed. "I'm very grateful for the whole library effort because the library was something I had a strong personal benefit from, strong involvement with, and when you have a success like this where the librarians jump in and make it come together, it really motivates you to do more giving and even try some new and different things in giving.

"The biggest area for the foundation is health care in developing countries. There, the need is quite urgent, particularly around some of the epidemics, and yet we're very hopeful that, if the advances in science are applied to the needs of the world at large, we can come up with vaccines and treatments. So I think that health giving will be the biggest part of the foundation's activity for quite some time, until we make some really big advances in the way we think about health for our children here in this country and the way parents in other countries think about their kids.

"In terms of libraries, we're talking with the various states. We are moving into a new phase. The whole training staff that we had, that did such a good job, has been delegated out to the various training centers we created. We hope that it sustains itself. We're doing some grants at the state level for sustaining it in the places where that will be the toughest.

"We are taking the library's program out to some other countries. You probably heard about what we did in Chile; that went very well. Of course, even the initial program included Canada, and so Canada basically is in the same situation as the United States, where you have pretty much 95% coverage—that is, 95% of libraries have internet access. And we've given some money to Mexico; that's in a fairly early stage. We did some in the United Kingdom, and we do expect to add countries. We really need to see a government that's very serious about libraries. It's not like you can just go to any country in the world and do a program, because the tradition of libraries and local library support actually is not that widespread. We see it in some countries that were part of the British Empire and some other places. But we'll push forward. We'd like to repeat the success in other locations.

READ MORE

Written by Bill Gates

- *Business @ the Speed of Thought: Succeeding in the Digital Economy* (with Collins Hemingway)
- *The Road Ahead* (with Nathan Myhrvold and Peter Rinearson)

"In terms of what's beyond, we don't really have a clear plan there, but health and education are pretty urgent needs. Certainly for our activity in the United States, I think the education-focused work, including scholarships and the focus on high schools, will be our biggest thing for some time to come. Melinda and I get very hands-on and involved in these things, and once we pick something, we like to see it through. The library effort is really the only thing where the foundation started something and, at least in terms of the initial goals, we feel like they were achieved and we almost feel nostalgic about the great things that went on."

Gates had said in 1998 that the goal of the project was that "anybody who can get to a library can get to the internet." I asked him if the goal had been achieved.

"Yes, to the 95% level, that goal has been achieved," he responded. "We came up with programs even for very small libraries. And you might have expected, okay, only half of the libraries would be interested, but the degree of interest was super-high. Less than 5% of the libraries weren't excited about participating in the training. You often see this with adults, who feel that kids understand computers better than they do; you see this a lot with teachers, who stay away from computers as much as they can because they're uncomfortable with them. Here—partly because librarians are so committed to their patrons, partly because the training was done in a way that drew them in—it got them to think about what people would be interested in. I think part of the principle of being a librarian is you want people to have access to information, so the program really appealed to how librarians thought of their role. The participation was phenomenal, way beyond what we would have expected.

"I didn't realize that librarians are often working without much acknowledgment of the important role they play. The program was valuable in terms of adding this new tool to the library, but also giving the librarians a chance to remind people of the central role that the library has in the community and the fact that staying up-to-date requires a sustained commitment from people in the community for the library to play that role.

"During the program, I got out to a library in South Dakota because Tom Brokaw grew up there. His process of randomly testing whether we really were covering the libraries was to assume that we hadn't done something in his obscure hometown [Yankton]. So we actually went to that area and met with the patrons and the librarians. I have seen how libraries are particularly strong in rural communities," he said.

But Gates said the computerization project in rural communities had not been well reported on by the media. "I'm kind of disappointed in the way it got covered. There was a *New York Times* article that acted like our goal was to move people out of rural areas. It was unfortunate that the *New York Times* article took that angle. The fact that people who stay in rural areas can stay in touch with people and get at information sources they wouldn't otherwise have, that's just a fantastic thing. The whole role of the library in these rural communities is amazing. It's an organization point for a lot of community activities, and it's super-neat. The internet connection has actually helped reinforce that."

Gates said he was also disappointed that the project "hasn't gotten more visibility—not that there haven't been articles that have overstressed the filtering issue or any of the controversial issues. I wish that there was an even broader awareness [of the library computerization program], because that's very important for the sustainability that is going to be determined community by community."

When the American Library Association awarded Honorary Membership to the Gateses in 1998, there was muttering in some sectors of the organization about Bill Gates's motivation for the massive computerization effort. I asked him how he responded to skeptics who said the foundation's library program was a marketing ploy to make permanent Microsoft customers out of public libraries and their patrons.

"That was a criticism that we expected," he said. "There's probably somebody who got exposed to the software in the library and chose to buy a personal computer. But it was not the reason that the program was done. I think computer literacy for society is a very positive thing, particularly not having it be something only for the wealthiest in society or just the people in big cities. The fact that overall exposure to computers and software might have a benefit to the industry, I think that's a fairly small thing and it wasn't the key motivation. But I can't deny that someone might have been excited about software after using it in the library and ended up buying a computer.

"I think a lot of that criticism has gone away as people have seen that the foundation embraces a broad set of have-versus-have-not issues, both in the United States and on a global basis. When you're going to do philanthropy, you don't do it expecting to get all positive exposure. You'd better have a model in your

Every time I get a chance to see what's going on and meet the librarians, meet the patrons, it's been just an incredible thing. The statistics are pretty good, but it's the anecdotes that just draw you in. By using a computer in the library, there's somebody who found a job or stayed in touch with a relative or learned something they didn't think they'd ever learn. — BILL GATES

own mind and a trust in your own mind that what you're doing has a very positive effect," he added.

I reminded Gates that back in 1998 he had said that if he had to choose between computers and books, he would choose books. "Do you still feel that way?" I asked, "and how do you instill that love of reading and libraries in your own children?"

"I spent the weekend doing a reading-training thing with my 4-year-old, and my 7-year-old just finished reading this book, *Holes*, which is actually, for her, a pretty big book, and it was a long book and she was worried when she started, it had so many pages. But anyway, she finally got it done. And we didn't let her watch the movie until after she'd read the book, and so she celebrated by watching the movie. But then we got her started on a new book.

"There are some neat things happening in reading, whether it's teaching phonics through software in some neat ways, or these accelerated-reading activities: after kids read a book they can show that they have proficiency with what was in the book, and it gives them positive feedback.

"Part of the thing about being so busy in my job and foundation work is that I love to read, but I don't get as much time as I'd like. My latest vacation, I got to read 10 books. I really enjoyed it and had a lot of fun, a real treat.

"My kids will love reading books, and there's a lot of data about how, the more you read, it's a predictor of success. You get curiosity that allows you to be a very good citizen and participate in lifelong learning.

"The fact is, there's no computers-versus-books dichotomy. That's been very well established by some of the data that's come out in the libraries program. In the years that the program has moved forward, more people have come to the library. The people who came for the computers use the books. The people who came for the books use the computers. So it's not this one-versus-the-other type thing. I feel very good about that. I didn't feel there would be much risk of that, but the University of Washington, which we funded to do a lot of in-depth follow-up, says the data are very much on the high, positive end of what I would have hoped for.

"Every time I get a chance to see what's going on and meet the librarians, meet the patrons, it's been just an incredible thing. The statistics are pretty good, but it's the anecdotes that just draw you in. By using a computer in the library, there's somebody who found a job or stayed in touch with a relative or learned something they didn't think they'd ever learn. It's all the stuff that makes me love my job in terms of creating software and love the fact that I've had a chance to help out in this way through the foundation."

I revisited those Alabama libraries—Montgomery, Selma, and Demopolis—in 2003 to assess the impact and sustainability of the nearly $180 million the Bill and Melinda Gates Foundation invested in libraries since the project was launched. The goal of "anybody who can get to a library can get to the internet" had been achieved, Alabama State Librarian Rebecca Mitchell told me. "It's taken us into the next century." Every county in Alabama has access to the internet in its public libraries, she said, and that would not be so without the Gates gift. "The digital divide has been seriously bridged," she added, with at least one library in every one of the state's 67 counties offering access and most with multiple access points, "so every citizen has access to the Web."

"Our door count tripled," said Lindsy Gardner, then director of the Demopolis Public Library. "It made a huge impact and still does." The library offers the only free internet access in the area, and that "gave the library a cutting-edge image" and "shone a light on libraries that we have tried to keep shining."

For the past five years, said Becky Nichols, then director and children's librarian at the Selma–Dallas County Public Library, the computers have been so busy so much of the time that the staff can't keep an accurate user count. Computers have resulted in increasing traffic patterns for programs and books as well, she added.

Although then Montgomery City-County Public Library director Juanita Owes was cautious about pronouncing the digital divide officially closed, she believed that "the community at poverty level knows the library is here for them." Ostensibly named for the rich quality of its earth, the Black Belt has also come to stand for the largely African-American population that lives there. As the director of a public library that was off-limits to her as a black child growing up in the segregated South, Owes was especially aware of the weighty responsibility for equitable access.

And what about those skeptics who said the whole effort was a marketing plan?

"If it was a marketing plan, it was a good one," quipped Owes, "and I don't know anyone who doesn't agree."

"I don't ever look a gift horse in the mouth," said Nichols. "I'm too busy being grateful." She thought the cynicism was a sign of the times, "a sign that we don't trust anyone and can't see something good and decent for what it was meant to be: generosity of spirit."

"If we had not had the support from the Gates Foundation, considering economic conditions in Alabama," said Mitchell, "we would still have the great digital divide." ★

DAVID MAMET

playwright, screenwriter, film director

4

GETTING AN EDUCATION

"My alma mater is the Chicago Public Library."

The Chicago Public Library Foundation marked its 20th anniversary in 2006 with a fund-raiser honoring David Mamet that garnered a record $525,000 in support for the library. Presented with the Carl Sandburg Literary Award, Mamet credited the library and the education he received in the reading room of the old central library (now the Chicago Cultural Center) for his accomplishments as a writer. Some 500 library supporters attended the bash in the Harold Washington Library Center's grand Winter Garden atrium, including Chicago Mayor Richard M. Daley, who received a Library Champion Award for "his strong personal commitment to and advocacy for Chicago's libraries and reading."

Born in 1947 in Chicago, Illinois, Mamet first gained recognition as a playwright for a trio of off-Broadway plays in 1976: *The Duck Variations*, *Sexual Perversity in Chicago*, and *American Buffalo*.

Photo by Vera Anderson for WireImage, courtesy of Getty Images.

He was awarded the Pulitzer Prize in 1984 for his play *Glengarry Glen Ross*. He received Academy Award nominations for his film scripts for *The Verdict* (1982) and *Wag the Dog* (1997).

"He's known to be reclusive with regard to public appearances and difficult to interview once he's been nabbed," said a library press release, "so of course that tends to make one particularly curious to hear whether this highly talented writer might indeed offer some pearls of wisdom." I was, so I attended the small cocktail party in his honor before the program and was able to speak with Mamet, briefly. He was serious and indeed rather reticent. He told me that everything he had accomplished as a writer was the result of the time he spent at the library and that he considered the Chicago Public Library his alma mater.

I didn't take him literally and wondered what kind of speech he would give. Taking my place in the audience, I never imagined I would hear one of America's most celebrated writers say that he had learned the essential elements of his craft at the Chicago Public Library. The next day, I contacted the library and asked if we could publish Mamet's speech in its entirety. There was very little that an interview could have added. This is what we ended up publishing in *American Libraries*.

MY ALMA MATER is the Chicago Public Library. I got what little educational foundation I got in the third-floor reading room, under the tutelage of a Coca-Cola sign. I somehow came across a copy of *Main Street*, and I was stunned to find descriptions of things and emotions I had seen and felt—the wind on the prairies, a longing.

I came to the library as a young man, wandering in the open stacks. I read all of Sinclair Lewis, and a book jacket mentioned Willa Cather, so I read all of Willa Cather, and then another book

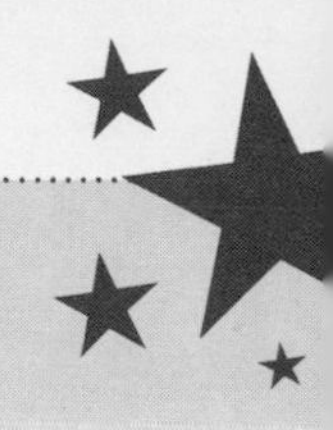

I cut school and came downtown to sit at the long tables and read. It didn't feel to me like education, and the novels, I came to realize later, didn't feel to me like literature . . . — DAVID MAMET

took me to another Midwestern writer, and then to the Chicago writers. Theodore Dreiser became and remains my hero. He wrote about those things that I, as a young man, was experiencing every day—loneliness, the need to find work, to make money, to fight my way in, in short, to understand.

The spirit of Chicago permeated those books: Frank Norris writing about the Mercantile Exchange, Willa Cather about the arts, Ralph Ellison and Richard Wright on the particular struggle of African Americans, Philip Roth and Saul Bellow on the particular plight of the Jews.

These stories read to me like the best of American news writing: who, what, where, when, and how. Like the newspaper, they were stories, in the main, about the working people, about living in a worker's town.

I sat in the reading room and read the novels, for that's all I read, one after another, three or four in a Saturday afternoon. I cut school and came downtown to sit at the long tables and read.

It didn't feel to me like education, and the novels, I came to realize later, didn't feel to me like literature, the awarding of which appellation is, I understand, the province of education. The horror of my life, in those days, was "the Chicago Public Schools Report Card, Benjamin C. Willis, Superintendent." The report card was in a buff envelope similar to those glued into the back of the books I read at the public library and in that other

The library is, and always has been, our national schoolhouse. — DAVID MAMET

great venue of education, the Chicago Transit Authority. And those great Chicago stories were associated with the particular sway of the el train, the cigarette smoke and the fumes on the buses, the hot radiator and urine stink of the waiting rooms on the Illinois Central Railroad. My heroes were and are the free-thinkers, the shade-tree mechanics or philosophers, who stripped it down to the metal and could explain their ideas in a paragraph: Clarence Darrow, Thorstein Veblen, Vachel Lindsay, Abraham Lincoln, who walked these actual streets. Chicago, it was said in the years after the Civil War, was the first American city.

I think that we in Chicago, in our love of our heritage, have something more of the European about us. When I was a kid we all pointed out the corner of Holy Name Cathedral where the shots went wild when they tried to get Dion O'Bannion, the spot on Clark Street where they threw the St. Valentine's Day Massacre, the place in Lincoln Park where the police started taking names in 1968. And the readers remember the stone lions outside the library from Willard Motley's *Knock on Any Door*, the Fine Arts Building featured in both Dreiser and Cather, the bridges cropping up in every novel of a hundred years, and Philip Roth in *Letting Go*, who reminds us that everything—proposal, divorce, meditation, recrimination, confession—takes place at the lake.

Thomas Jefferson said that given the choice of government without newspapers or newspapers without a government he would choose the latter, for the newspaper was the abstract and brief chronicle of its time.

I fear that 220 years on, it is less so. The amalgamation of the press and its horizontal and vertical integration into that which we know as the "media" have weakened the intellectual life of the country. By intellectual I do not mean writers such as myself and academics pontificating, but rather the free flow of ideas. For the American people are pretty good at the free exchange of ideas.

My dad loved Chicago in that quiet way most of us do, as a man loves his family. If you asked him, "Do you love your family?" he might look at you askance, and respond, "Well, of course." And Chicago, my dad always made the point, was a workers' town.

The workers—and if I may, we workers—have always been rather good at the free exchange of ideas. On the job, we most probably do not know the political orientation of the man or woman next to us, and we would consider it impolite to inquire. We observe their character—that is to say, simply, we watch how they behave and we form our opinions of them based on that

READ MORE

Recommended by DAVID MAMET

- ★ ***Knock on Any Door,*** by Willard Motley
- ★ ***Letting Go,*** by Philip Roth
- ★ ***Main Street,*** by Sinclair Lewis
- ★ The works of Saul Bellow, Willa Cather, Clarence Darrow, Theodore Dreiser, Ralph Ellison, Abraham Lincoln, Vachel Lindsay, Frank Norris, and Richard Wright

good test: How are they on the job? And if they comment on the political situation, that comment is most likely couched with reserve and without partisanship. For on the job, we know we have to work together, and we discuss the world around us, searching for the unity of opinion, stating our ideas with reserve, open to new interpretation.

This is a great, great country we live in, and it was and is built by simple working people with a better idea: George Pullman, Harriet Tubman, Muddy Waters, Bill Gates, Thomas Edison, Henry Ford, Louis B. Mayer, Abraham Lincoln, the common people whose better ideas were adopted by their fellows—sometimes after monumental strife—and went on to influence the world.

America is not a melting pot, thank God. Those of us with a racial, a religious, a geographic heritage love and revere that heritage, as is correct. It's called filial piety, and it makes the country strong. It's not a melting pot, but it is a laboratory. And since our revolution it has been the laboratory of the world.

How did it become so? Through the free exchange of free ideas. Every advance, every innovation in industry, science, or art, builds upon the work of those who have gone before, which is the common store. That worth, that common store, is the library.

READ MORE

written by DAVID MAMET

- ★ *American Buffalo*
- ★ *The Duck Variations*
- ★ *Glengarry Glen Ross*
- ★ *Sexual Perversity in Chicago*

The media exists to enflame us, and I hold no brief—at least in the liberal arts—for that which calls itself Higher Education. The library is, and has always been, our national schoolhouse.

At a dark point several years ago, the government sent up a trial balloon: It announced it was considering obtaining all the records of all bookstores to see who was reading what. An acquaintance of mine, owner of a bookstore in Montpelier, Vermont, took his files into the parking lot and burned them. This, to me, was a profound and courageous statement, for when and if the government controls what we can read, America, as we have known it, is finished. And it makes no difference if the particular government inquiring is or seems benign—once we establish that principle, once we make the American people afraid to read, the laboratory of the world is dead.

The computer presents itself as a tool of increased literacy and communication. The jury is out. It may very well prove, in retrospect, to have been the death of both literacy and communication, for if information can be centrally controlled (and it seems it can), it can and most probably will be altered.

The information on the computer is just electrons, or whatever they are, on a screen. Where might one go to find out if the information is correct, to seek out an opposing view? To the library—an uncontrolled, nonjudgmental, open, inviting compendium of wisdom.

My highest desire as a kid was to write. It never occurred to me that books I had written could take their place alongside those of my heroes, but it seems that that has come to pass, and I must thank the institution which then, for me, and now, for others, makes such accomplishment possible. ★

LAURA BUSH

former First Lady of the United States, author, philanthropist

5

FIRST LIBRARIAN

"My favorite thing to do is to read."

Librarian and teacher Laura Bush remained true to her profession for eight years in the White House, as First Lady to President George W. Bush.

The First Lady is likely to be best remembered for her love of books and for what that love inspired, including her own children's book, *Read All About It!* coauthored with her daughter Jenna Bush Hager. "It's about a little boy who loves everything, he rules the school, but he doesn't particularly like to read," Mrs. Bush explained to me during an interview at the White House in March 2008. "And it's dedicated to all little boys like that and to the teachers who just persistently keep reading those stories and sharing those books with them until children find out they do love those stories and they do love to read."

In some ways, Laura Bush's eight years as First Lady of the United States were a counterbalance to her husband's presidency. Consistently popular, even while President Bush's approval ratings rose and fell, she maintained an independent public persona.

Photo by Shealah Craighead, courtesy of the White House.

In 2006, *People* magazine asked Laura Bush how she felt when her husband was being criticized. She used it as an opportunity to plug libraries: "I don't like that," she said, "but we've been involved [in politics] for years. When you go to the Lincoln Library in Springfield, Illinois, and see what political cartoons and pamphlets said about President Lincoln, you see that it's not worse. People are the same no matter what generation."

It was the combination of reading and children that made a librarian out of Laura Bush to begin with, she said. "I loved kids; I loved being with them. But what I loved best was sharing literature with them—reading stories with them and teaching them to read." So she decided after three years of teaching to go back to graduate school for a degree in library science, then worked for a year for Houston Public Library, and then moved to Austin and went back to a school library, "just really wanting to be in a school with kids all the time."

That same love of children and reading is at the heart of the initiatives and programs she supported throughout her years in the White House, from "Ready to Read, Ready to Learn" in 2001 to the 2008 White House Symposium on Advancing Global Literacy.

The first time I talked with Laura Bush was at a small luncheon in 2007 at the National Museum of Women in the Arts in Washington, where she hosted a book launch for daughter Jenna's *Ana's Story*, a work of narrative nonfiction about HIV-AIDS. Seated at the same table, I was able to chat with Mrs. Bush and Jenna through lunch. She had recently visited the Library of Alexandria in Egypt, and so had I, so we shared memories and our amazement at the magnitude of the project. The First Lady was a listener.

After lunch, she gave a short speech praising librarians and introducing her daughter, who reflected on the UNICEF internship she had just completed, documenting the lives of children in Latin America who are excluded from basic care and education.

When lunch was over, Mrs. Bush shook hands and posed for photos with her guests. As she held my hand, I popped the question: Would you give *American Libraries* an exclusive interview? She didn't miss a beat: "I'd like that very much," she said and instructed me to contact her press secretary to make the arrangements.

On March 19, 2008, I arrived at the White House press room with a camera crew. Mrs. Bush was ushered in and greeted us. We took our places on delicate antique chairs, surrounded by books. I tried to break the ice by saying that I sometimes joke that I was born a librarian. "Were you born a librarian?" I asked.

Mrs. Bush smiled indulgently and said, "Well, I was born to love to read, I think, partly because my mother read to me, as she says, from when my eyes opened. And that made a huge difference in my life, an unbelievable difference. I mean, my favorite thing to do is to read."

I asked her if her training and experience as a librarian and teacher translate into the White House, if it helped prepare her in any way. It was the one question I asked that seemed genuinely to surprise her.

"It really did, and I would have never really thought of it before," she said, "but both the experience I had of reading to

If you are a high-tech kid, young person, and want to think about a job where you could use that to a big advantage, and really to expand people's access to knowledge, then a library is that place to be. — LAURA BUSH

children over and over and over, and storytelling, were really excellent training for giving speeches. And I would have never thought of that or translated it that way. But then also, both when George was governor and now since he's been president, all the issues that surround literacy—education, even economic power, economic advantage—all the advantages that a good reader has over a nonreader end up being very, very important issues in our country, both for school policy issues as well as so many other issues, including international issues: the rights of women to go to school, to be educated—all the things that we've seen over the last few years in other countries where people are denied an education, and we know how important they are. So all of that experience has been hugely helpful to me."

I asked her to talk about the 21st-century library education grants, and why the recruitment of new library and information science professionals is so important.

"We know from the numbers that as the Boomers age, we're going to lose a lot of librarians," she said, "and it's very important for us to reach out to young people, to let them know what working in the library is really like. We know that we suffer from the very worst stereotype, and it's always been that way."

I asked her to pretend that I was a twentysomething graduate from college and convince me that I should become a librarian.

"I think there's a really exciting case to make for libraries," she replied. "First, they're filled with all information. They're filled with any kind of information you might want. Second, they are now very high-tech. And if you are a high-tech kid, young person, and want to think about a job where you could use that to a big advantage, and really to expand people's access to knowledge, then a library is that place to be.

"If you're a people person, libraries are a great place to be, because you work with people all day. You're working with people and information. And one of the things I loved best when I was an intern at Austin Public Library in graduate school was just working the reference desk at night and having people come in and ask about whatever their interest was. And that always interested me. And in many cases, it would be something I knew nothing about. But just helping them find the research materials on it gave me one other really interesting topic that I could be interested in myself."

I reminded her that she had once said, "Reading is the foundation for all learning," and asked her how librarians can better leverage the empirical evidence—what we know are the facts and the studies that have shown that reading is good exercise for the brain.

"I think especially school librarians have a role to play in getting that message out," she said, "but I think librarians—and I know you all discuss this, probably, at conferences—really need to do a lot more outreach. They need to let people know both how important libraries are, and how important reading is.

"I got a letter once, when George was governor, from a person in San Angelo, who said the advantages of a reader are so profound, so many over the nonreader, that people ought to be demanding to learn to read. And I think that really is true, and I think we see it in countries where people are denied an education, that they're desperate for an education, they're desperate to learn to read.

"So I think that's what we need to get out. That not only should we offer, in every library if we can, literacy classes or literacy—different vehicles for learning to read—because of all the people in our country, immigrants who maybe don't read English or the people who've made it through school without learning to read. One thing all of us know is that there are plenty of people out there who don't read. And we should really do whatever we can to reach out to people and let them know that there are ways to learn to read."

I asked Mrs. Bush when she became a reader, if she remembered the moment. I had read that Laura Ingalls Wilder's books were an important early reading experience for her, as they were for me.

"She was a favorite of mine, for sure," she recalled, "and my mother started reading *The Little House on the Prairie* to me before I could read. But I do remember when I first read it. But actually, the book that I remember first being able to read for myself was *Mrs. Piggle-Wiggle.* I don't know if you remember the *Mrs. Piggle-Wiggle* books," she laughed. "They're sort of not in fashion any more. But I had a very good friend who was an excellent reader, a better reader than I was. I was younger, I started school at five, started school early, and as I look back on it, I was a little bit behind in development compared to—not everyone—but many of my classmates. And she and I would lie on the couch and she would read *Mrs. Piggle-Wiggle.* And then all of a sudden I realized I could read. And it probably was the 2nd or 3rd grade."

The National Book Festival and many of Laura Bush's initiatives as First Lady focused on books. I asked her why and to speculate on the future of the book.

"Books are so important to me, and I think they're so important to a democracy and so important to our society that it just seems natural that we would try to promote books in any way we could. I mean, it's just been the cause of my life, as you know. It's been the pleasure of my life, reading. And I made what I like to do best into my job, which was a librarian, a teacher and a librarian.

"So the book festivals themselves are really a celebration of what I like best and what I hope every American, and especially young people, will also learn to like: reading and books.

"We started the Texas Book Festival after an author from El Paso brought the idea to me. He had been invited to a book festival in Kentucky some years ago, where the First Lady of Kentucky had a coffee or a reception for the authors. He thought it was a great idea. So we put together a very great committee—with a lot of Texas writers on it—and developed the Texas Book Festival. And it was just fun. I mean, it was really one of the most pleasurable activities I had—the chance to meet authors whose works I'd read and admired for years. And the Texas Book Festival is a fund-raiser for Texas public libraries, which is difficult. It's difficult to raise the amount of money you need to produce a big festival and have money left over to be able to give away. But we've been very successful at it.

"But all of those things are great fun, and the National Book Festival has been a huge success. More than 120,000 people came to the National Book Festival last year on the mall, and that's more people than are in the town where I grew up."

I broached the topic of censorship by asking, "What do we say to parents who want to keep their children from what they think is inappropriate material by having it pulled from the library shelves?"

"I think parents have a very important role," she said. "The books that our mothers or our fathers chose to read to us when we were little shaped our lives, they really did. And I think that's what parents should think about, what they can pick. First, be sure they do read to their children every day, especially their

READ MORE
Recommended by LAURA BUSH

- ★ ***Ana's Story: A Journey of Hope,*** by Jenna Bush
- ★ ***The Brothers Karamazov,*** by Fyodor Dostoyevsky
- ★ ***The Little House books,*** by Laura Ingalls Wilder
- ★ ***Mrs. Piggle-Wiggle,*** by Betty MacDonald

preschool children, but keep reading the center of your family life for your whole life. And if you think there are books that are inappropriate, there are certainly things you can do. You could go to your child's school if it's something that's in the child's school, or talk, I would suggest in private, with the librarian or with the teacher.

"But I also think that parents can have a very profound effect on what their children choose to read, and teachers and librarians can too, and that is by offering a wide variety of interesting books that really make a difference, that have made a difference in their own lives. I also think you have to offer a wide variety of books on motorcycles and dinosaurs, too, for those boys who think they don't want to read," she laughed.

Media speculation about his reading habits notwithstanding, President Bush's budget did, in fact, include an increase for libraries every year of his administration. I asked if she had influenced her husband to make this happen.

"Well, no, I would say no. I probably really haven't. But I have stayed very close and interested with both of our Institute of Museum and Library Services directors. We've had terrific

People don't realize how expensive a whole library collection is. A basic elementary collection probably costs about $50,000, a start-up collection. And, of course, a high school library could cost $150,000 or more.

— LAURA BUSH

ones: Robert Martin, who is a librarian himself, for the first four years, and then Anne Radice, who is the IMLS director now, whose background is more with museums. And that's actually the way the heads of this agency are chosen, with a librarian first, and then alternating, library and museum person. But also I hosted a summit, early on in George's first term, on school libraries and how important they are to schools. And so I've had a very effective and close relationship with IMLS, which has been good. And then of course, it's always very important to have people on the Hill, because that's where the money is actually appropriated. And both the president and I have friends on the Hill who take libraries very seriously and believe that they should have more money."

"What do you think needs to happen for the success of No Child Left Behind?" I asked. It was the only one of my questions that got something of a rise out of the First Lady.

"No Child wasn't reauthorized—which I'm disappointed about, and maybe that will happen later this year; I hope so. But Margaret Spellings, the secretary of education, is working on some rules of flexibility for school districts that will take care of some of the things we were hoping would be in a reauthorization.

"But also I think it's really important for the accountability piece to stay there. I know that there are some parts of No Child Left Behind that have been hugely successful according to the new research that we now have on how people learn to read—the Reading First part, where school districts offer reading instruction for all their kindergarten teachers, for instance, or all their 1st-grade teachers or all their 2nd-grade teachers. And actually, scores are up. They're higher than they've ever been in reading and math among 4th-graders, among the young people who have been learning to read and do math since No Child Left Behind has been in effect."

I continued: "How do you respond to the critics who say that it fosters teaching to the test?"

"If what you want your children to know is to read and to do math, then that's what you should test them on," she asserted, "and I think that is what the curriculum should be. And in fact—and I don't know that everyone knows this—each state writes its own curriculum. And that's what they want their children in the state to know. And if your curriculum is what you want your children to know, and that's what you teach, then your children should do well on the accountability test.

"Another criticism I've heard is that all the teachers are doing is teaching reading. Well, what are you having children read? If you have a really rich curriculum with a lot of really good subjects in it and books in it, and you're teaching children to read them, then that is a good basic education, and that's what we want. And it turns out that most teachers in elementary school and all the way through high school need to teach reading. If you're a history teacher, you're teaching vocabulary, you're teaching words that have to do with your subject. If you're a science teacher, you're doing the same thing. I think that if people and teachers are all aware of that, children end up with a much richer and broader education."

I asked Mrs. Bush to talk about the priorities of the Laura Bush Foundation for America's Libraries and how those are set, including the fact that the foundation had awarded $3.7 million

READ MORE

WRITTEN BY LAURA BUSH

- ★ *Read All About It!* (with Jenna Bush)
- ★ *Spoken from the Heart*

for hurricane-stricken schools and the rebuilding of libraries in those schools.

"All during the presidential campaign, and really while George was governor as well, I visited schools. Usually if I visited a school in a more affluent area, I visited a great school library. But I remember one in particular in Newark, where the school library had half a dozen books. And they were all the same atlas that was totally out of date, or a reference book that was 10 years old. And so it made me aware of how important it was for school libraries to have money to buy materials."

The Laura Bush Foundation for America's Libraries was established in 2002 and awarded its first grants the following year. "Those went to school libraries," Mrs. Bush explained. "They're not big grants; they're $5,000 to $10,000, but in many cases they double the school library budget for books for that year. And the grants are written to ask for something specific, whatever they might need that supports the curriculum or supports the school body population, maybe books in Spanish."

In 2005, following the devastation of Hurricane Katrina, the foundation turned its attention to raising money for schools across the Gulf Coast to rebuild their library collections.

"We've now given over $3 million," Mrs. Bush said, to some 52 schools across the Gulf Coast. "And these are big amounts of money, from $50,000 to $150,000 for whole collections, because people don't realize how expensive a whole library collection is. A basic elementary collection probably costs about $50,000, a start-up collection. And, of course, a high school library could cost $150,000 or more."

As the interview drew to a close, I asked Mrs. Bush to talk about what comes after the White House and to talk about her role in her husband's presidential library.

"Oh, I will have a role in his presidential library," she said confidently. "I'm really looking forward to being actively involved in the building of it. We have a very good architect. And as you know, presidential libraries work with the National Archives and Records Administration, to develop everything that surrounds the papers, including the conservation and the temperature control that any archivist knows about, and then of course also the regular access to it, and the ways that the papers are cataloged and put together.

"I'm also interested in the ideas that [the president] has behind the library, which is an institute for freedom. People from around the world that we've met and admire—like Vaclav Havel, a freedom fighter from the Czech Republic, from the former Czechoslovakia—would have a chance to come and work there and work on their own papers and write about it.

"So I think there will be a very good opportunity for me to continue all the things I've already done around libraries and literacy, working out of that library, and continuing to work in the United States, and then on the international issues that I think are also very important—the ideas of international global literacy and especially the gender differences that have kept many women from being educated."

Half jokingly, I asked her if she had ever thought about running for public office. She looked at me as if I'd suggested she start selling drugs.

"No, I won't be running for public office," she assured me. What she was looking forward to was getting back to their old hometown of Crawford, Texas, where she could devote her time to "a lot of different issues."

"I just want to thank all your readership," Mrs. Bush added. "I want to thank librarians who work every single day to make sure people have access to every kind of information—for free. And I think that's just very, very important. It's important for our country, and it's important for democracy, and it's just very personally important for individuals." ★

KEN BURNS

documentary filmmaker

6

ARCHIVING AMERICA

"I don't think that there has been a film that I've done that hasn't been influenced by libraries and archives."

"We're so excited to be here at ALA and share with our peeps the most important work we've done," said Ken Burns when I finally made my way into his busy schedule at the American Library Association's Annual Conference in Washington in 2007. It had been especially important that Burns speak that year because his latest documentary film, *The War*, was about to be released and we could preview it at the conference. His reputation as America's finest documentary filmmaker had already been established with films such as *Baseball*, *Jazz*, and *Unforgivable Blackness*, which had aired on public television. It was, however, the research, as opposed to the final product, that intrigued me. Burns would surely have much to say about the reading and research in the libraries and archives that preceded the production of these great films.

In making arrangements for his appearance, I was in frequent touch with Burns through his staff, and he agreed to write an original article for *American Libraries* delineating how he did his

Photo by Cable Risdon.

research. I didn't know what to expect, but he met his deadline and we published the piece in the June-July issue, just in time for the conference. Here is what he wrote.

I DON'T REMEMBER A TIME when I wasn't interested in making films. From my earliest days, my father gave me a fairly strict curfew, but he'd always forgive it if there was a movie on TV late at night or something playing at the Cinema Guild. My interest in history is a little bit more difficult to pinpoint.

Though I had always done well in history throughout school, it wasn't until many, many years later—after I had established my career—that I was stopped by an old junior high school classmate who remembered me from history class and said, "I always looked at you and knew that's what you wanted to do."

If you had asked me in 9th grade what I wanted to do, I would have said a writer or a filmmaker. History was the farthest thing from my imagination. But it turned out my classmate was right.

Today, we're well aware of how important nutrition is. I think we know that if we eat well, if we exercise, we help stave off the inevitable decay that takes place. I think we also understand that exercising the mind, which is constantly evolving, is probably the healthiest of all of the things we can do for ourselves. The key to that is for people to understand that we're not just coasting here. We almost have an obligation to keep learning.

Thomas Jefferson said in his famous second sentence of the Declaration of Independence that we were entitled to "Life, Liberty, and the pursuit of Happiness," and for most people that means a pursuit of material goods. I know that Jefferson, by saying capital-H "Happiness," meant a kind of lifelong learning, an improving of oneself in the marketplace of ideas, and that any citizen first given life and liberty was then obligated to continue to improve oneself, to work on oneself, for the rest of one's life. It was the *pursuit* of happiness—not something that we'd actually achieve—and so it suggests a lifelong quest for self-improvement, which, to my mind, is not just physical, but also mental and emotional.

I don't think that there has been a film that I've done that hasn't been influenced by libraries and archives, and therefore my whole life is essentially organized and categorized by what they make available. That's what I do for a living: I'm kind of an emotional archaeologist. For instance, with *The War* we wanted to take an entirely anecdotal, bottom-up look at the Second World War, and to do that, we picked four geographically distributed towns, got to know those towns, accepted whatever and whomever came up to us, and then proceeded to research, film, and interview before intertwining the various stories and setting them against the greatest cataclysm in human history.

So, as I go to these places, I'm not just trying to unearth the dry dates and facts and events of the past—things that have so little meaning to us now in our distracting, glittering present—but I'm interested in using the emotional resonances of that past, whether it's through a photograph, or a diary excerpt, or just a startling fact. While making the *Civil War* series, I found out that the little town of Winchester, Virginia, changed hands 72 times,

READ MORE

Recommended by KEN BURNS

★ ***The Road to Home: My Life and Times,*** by Vartan Gregorian

and that fact has never left me for its startling power to remind us that, at a time not that long ago, parts of the United States were not only a battleground, but suffered that much of a back-and-forth struggle.

Another example from *The Civil War*: I was at the Museum of the Confederacy in Richmond, Virginia, and I asked them if they had a box of "seconds"—materials that hadn't been properly cataloged. The curator said yes, and he brought out a box literally filled with dozens of mostly duplicates of what I'd already seen.

But I spent about an hour searching, and at the bottom, stuck under a flap, was a photograph. It showed Robert E. Lee with a kind of winsome, Mona Lisa–like smile—and you must understand that in mid-19th-century photographs no one ever smiled. I looked up and said, "I've never seen this photograph before," and the curator said, "Neither have I." At that moment, you know you're in archival heaven, and you thank God for libraries and historical societies every day of your life.

We used to have a joke that there were two kinds of archivists: one who kept her collection in apple-pie order and was thrilled to share it with the rest of the world, and the other who

I looked up and said, "I've never seen this photograph before," and the curator said, "Neither have I." At that moment, you know you're in archival heaven, and you thank God for libraries and historical societies every day of your life. — KEN BURNS

The thing that we need to remember as a republic, is that these records are the DNA of who we are. And libraries and archives are where we stow and encode what future generations will interpret about us. — KEN BURNS

kept his collection in apple-pie order and would prefer it never to be touched. I believe, obviously, that the risk of a slight bit of attrition—the dog-eared corners; the minor rips; the, I'm sure, unfortunate disappearances of some items—is far outweighed by the value of allowing complete and total access by the public to materials.

I am mindful that nonprofit organizations—particularly archives and libraries—sometimes have to look for new streams of revenue, but sometimes these actions impede public access. On my first film, people were just so thrilled that anyone was interested in their collection that they would let us have access to the use of a particular photograph for free. That has changed almost across the board. There are now significant expenses connected with this process, and I think that it limits filmmaking.

When I was making a film back in the early 1980s on the Statue of Liberty and its history and symbolism, I had the great good fortune to meet and interview Vartan Gregorian, who was then the president of the New York Public Library in Manhattan. After this extremely fascinating interview with an immigrant—Vartan is from Tabriz, Iran—he said "Come on" and took me on a long and fascinating tour of the literally miles and miles of NYPL stacks. I chased this roly-poly man down one corridor after another.

Then he stopped, suddenly, in the middle of all of it, and he looked at me with this beaming smile on his face, like a child in a candy shop, and he said "this"—gesturing at his library from its guts—"this," he said, "is the DNA of our civilization."

I have never forgotten that. The thing that I appreciate, the thing that I like to remind people of, the thing that we need to remember as a republic, is that these records are the DNA of who we are. And libraries and archives are where we stow and encode what future generations will interpret about us. I can't imagine a better pursuit, I can't imagine a better place to spend a day, I can't imagine being able to thank those resources enough. ★

READ MORE

Written by KEN BURNS

- ★ *Baseball: An Illustrated History* (with Geoffrey C. Ward)
- ★ *The Civil War: An Illustrated History* (with Geoffrey C. Ward)
- ★ *Jazz: A History of America's Music* (with Geoffrey C. Ward)
- ★ *Mark Twain: An Illustrated Biography* (with Geoffrey C. Ward and Dayton Duncan)
- ★ *The National Parks: America's Best Idea* (with Dayton Duncan)
- ★ *The War: An Intimate History, 1941–1945* (with Geoffrey C. Ward)
- ★ *The West: An Illustrated History* (with Geoffrey C. Ward)

KAREEM ABDUL-JABBAR

basketball legend, coach, actor, author

7

FROM HOOPS TO INK

"Going to the library helped me understand how big the world was and the incredible amount of possibilities that you had for your life."

During an interview at the American Library Association's 2008 Midwinter Meeting in Philadelphia, Kareem Abdul-Jabbar told me, "I've been an avid reader my whole life and spent a lot of time in the library when I was a kid. It's nice to be associated with an organization like ALA."

The master of the sky hook, 7-foot-2-inches-tall Abdul-Jabbar led the University of California at Los Angles to three consecutive NCAA titles and the Milwaukee Bucks and the Los Angeles Lakers to six NBA championships.

Retired from sports, Abdul-Jabbar has authored or coauthored seven books—four of which made best-seller lists—including *Giant Steps*; *Black Profiles in Courage: A Legacy of African American Achievement*; *A Season on the Reservation: My Sojourn with the White Mountain Apache*; and *Brothers in Arms: The Epic Story of the 761st Tank Battalion, WWII's Forgotten Heroes.*

Abdul-Jabbar said he hoped that people who heard him speak and read his books would "get an idea that not all athletes

Photo by John Russo for the American Library Association.

who gain prominence are uneducated. I hope to show them that it does work in the other way too; that people can go through college and play athletics and get a first-rate education."

He described his role models, Jackie Robinson and Oscar Robertson, as two "great student athletes who went on to do great things as professionals," adding that "the whole idea of your education making you more of a man and more capable to give to society is something that all young people need to learn about."

Born Lew Alcindor in Harlem in 1947, the basketball legend turned author visited the American Library Association's headquarters in Chicago in December 2007, the day after being one of eight athletes inducted into the National Collegiate Hall of Fame established in 2006. Abdul-Jabbar talked with *American Libraries*

READ MORE
written by KAREEM ABDUL-JABBAR

- ★ *Black Profiles in Courage: A Legacy of African American Achievement* (with Alan Steinberg)
- ★ *Brothers in Arms: The Epic Story of the 761st Tank Battalion, WWII's Forgotten Heroes* (with Anthony Walton)
- ★ *Giant Steps* (with Peter Knobler)
- ★ *Kareem* (with Mignon McCarthy)
- ★ *On the Shoulders of Giants: My Journey through the Harlem Renaissance* (with Raymond Obstfeld)
- ★ *A Season on the Reservation: My Sojourn with the White Mountain Apache* (with Stephen Singular)

associate editor Pamela A. Goodes and me about his latest honor, and about libraries and reading.

"When I was in grade school I had no idea that I would become a professional athlete and college was about as high as you could aspire to. It was really neat to get the opportunity that I did at UCLA, and to even go further than that," he said.

We asked how he selected his book topics and if he used a library for his research.

"I certainly use the library for my research, but I select my topics based on my own gut feeling on what needs to be addressed and in what particular way it needs to be addressed. Everything that I've written has to do with my own personal life and experiences, so three of my books have been more or less autobiographical. I've also written three history books. My latest book on the Harlem Renaissance is both autobiography and history. For too many people, history is just dry facts, and a lot of people don't relate to it personally. If I can give my own personal connection to history, it makes it more accessible to people and enables them to relate better.

"James Baldwin's essays I found to be really fascinating and informative. They gave me a good perspective on what was going on in the Civil Rights Movement while I was growing up. Seeing something like that unfold while you're in high school can affect you in a lot of different ways, some of which could be very traumatic. The anger that was created by all the violence against black Americans trying to secure their civil rights was appalling. Having someone explain it to you and enable you to deal with it without becoming filled with hate and a need to retaliate really helped me a lot personally. I have to give credit to some of the people who were around—my high school coach Jack Donahue and other mentors who gave me a realistic perspective on it. I also read W. E. B. Du Bois and others who were in the Harlem Renaissance.

"When people take an active interest in what's going on now, they automatically will start looking at what happened, and you don't even have to go back as far as the Harlem Renaissance. The 1950s were a time of great turmoil in this country, if you look at what happened with the murder of Emmett Till. A lot can also be learned from Dr. King's efforts.

"Libraries are very important in helping young people get an understanding of how important it is to read. A lot of people don't have the money to buy books, and having a place where you can go and get a book, read it, and return it really enables you to broaden your perspective on life. Going to the library helped me understand how big the world was and the incredible amount of possibilities that you had for your life. Without the library, it wouldn't have been that obvious to me."

Abdul-Jabbar once taught basketball and history to American Indian children on a reservation. "I went to the White Mountain Apache Reservation in White River, Arizona, to do some research on the buffalo soldiers who were stationed at Fort Apache," he recalled. "I met members of the tribal council as well as the tribal historian, with whom I established a friendship. When they realized that I was interested in coaching, they asked if I could help with the boys basketball team and talk to some of them about going to college. Getting kids to go to college off the reservation is very difficult. There are a lot of cultural and socioeconomic pressures on them to never leave but they really need to do that to expand their world and to get the needed knowledge to do things for their tribe.

"Since I retired from professional basketball, I've tried to be involved with programs that promote literacy and learning. That's something that I feel is a key to advancement. No matter where you want to advance, no matter what field, literacy and learning really are part of it. Knowledge is power and if you're looking for the power to change, you have to make yourself

I'm coaching now for the Los Angeles Lakers and I deal with young men who are making millions of dollars a year, yet they are challenged to read a written page. And it hurts me. I don't want to see that they're not fully developed.

— KAREEM ABDUL-JABBAR

knowledgeable. This is a message I try to continually share with children and hope that it takes hold and they go out and learn how to change the world in a positive way."

Abdul-Jabbar's conference program in Philadelphia was a smash hit, focused largely on the giants of his latest book and topped off by an introduction to a library legend and civil rights champion, the late E. J. Josey.

Kicking off the question-and-answer session that followed, he said, "Please don't be shy. I'll talk to you about anything—even basketball," prompting laughter from the packed house.

Asked why he changed his name, he said, "My birth name was not good. I took the name Kareem Abdul-Jabbar when I accepted Islam—my family name was Alcindor, from the West Indies—and it all had to do with my spiritual conversion. Mohammed Ali took a lot of heat for all of us when he made the choice to change his name and I was very fortunate to come behind him and not have to deal with as much of it because of his sacrifice."

"How have tensions with Muslims in the United States changed since the Harlem Renaissance?" he was asked. He replied, "I certainly did not ever see any tension between Islam and American culture like we've had since 9/11. What's happened since 9/11 is unique in my mind. Muslims in America were a small minority and really were a blip on the map, in terms of the number of Muslims and their impact on American society—minimal. Then we have fanatics who come and do what they did and cause the pain and fear that's been part of the situation since 9/11. A lot of people don't know that a number of Muslims fought and died during the American Revolution. The French contingent under Lafayette had cavalry and infantry soldiers that fought during the last weeks of the American Revolutionary War; people aren't very much aware of that. The first country to recognize America as a sovereign nation was the kingdom of Morocco."

Asked what he would have done if he had been around during the Harlem Renaissance, Abdul-Jabbar replied, "Actually, it's very personal for me because my grandfather emigrated from the island of Trinidad and went to New York in 1917. He was part of the Great Migration to New York that created the Harlem Renaissance. So I can just imagine myself as my grandfather, walking the streets and being able to hear all this great music—the music of Fats Waller and Louis Armstrong. And I guess for me, person-

Going to the library helped me understand how big the world was and the incredible amount of possibilities that you had for your life. Without the library, it wouldn't have been that obvious to me. — KAREEM ABDUL-JABBAR

ally, I would have paid a lot more attention to my piano lessons," he said, chuckling.

"How can we get reluctant young people to read?" someone asked. He answered, "In trying to get young people to read, you have to be able to show them it's something that they need—it's something that will enhance them and make them more of what they want to be. A lot of young people don't understand that. They think whatever it is that they're focused on is all they need to do. I'm coaching now for the Los Angeles Lakers and I deal with young men who are making millions of dollars a year, yet they are challenged to read a written page. And it hurts me. I don't want to see that they're not fully developed."

Asked what his greatest basketball moment was, Abdul-Jabbar said, "I've been so blessed to have so many great basketball moments. As a professional athlete, for me, beating the Boston Celtics in 1985 was my greatest moment." Thunderous applause followed.

The audience at that program was filled with proud and grateful African-American librarians who believed that Kareem Abdul-Jabbar's leadership and activism is unparalleled in the history of race relations in the United States.

"You have always embodied the truest spirit of athletes," said E. J. Josey's son-in-law at the end of program, "and you have done it with grace and dignity." ★

COKIE ROBERTS

journalist, radio and television political commentator

8

A SENSE OF OUR FUTURE

"I've had wonderful experiences just calling up libraries and asking questions and getting the answers."

A political commentator for *ABC News* and senior news analyst for National Public Radio, Cokie Roberts, along with Sam Donaldson, co-anchored the ABC news program *This Week* from 1996 to 2002. With her husband Steven V. Roberts, she writes a syndicated weekly column that appears in newspapers around the country. She and her husband also coauthored *From This Day Forward*, an account of their decades-long marriage (now more than 40 years) and other marriages in American history. Cokie Roberts is also the author of the best sellers *Founding Mothers* and its companion volume *Ladies of Liberty*. In 2008 HarperCollins published *We Are Our Mothers' Daughters*, a 10th-anniversary edition of Roberts's *New York Times* best seller.

I interviewed Roberts by telephone and again in the green room before her program at the 2009 ALA Annual Conference in Chicago. I told her over the telephone that I was nervous about interviewing

Photo by Susan Watts for NY Daily News, courtesy of Getty Images.

one of America's legendary interviewers. Super cool and confident, she laughed and said, "Let's just have a conversation."

In *We Are Our Mothers' Daughters*, Roberts writes about women succeeding in professions that were traditionally considered the domain of men. I asked how she was able to develop the confidence and determination it took to do so.

"I was raised by parents who thought you could do anything you wanted to do," she said, "and I also was lucky as a girl in the 1950s—when a lot of people were basically telling girls they couldn't do much of anything—to be educated by a very intellectual order of nuns who also had made it very clear that not only could you do anything, but you were expected to do a good deal."

Considering Roberts's successful career devoted to the human record, I wanted to know what she thought about its future. "What do you think are the implications for the human record as more of it moves online and more newspapers are in trouble?" I asked.

"It's something that we spend a huge amount of time trying to figure out," she said. "It's not just the preservation of the re-

Anytime I walk into a library it is lively and full of people and lots of kids and there are all kinds of notices tacked up to the bulletin board, there are community gatherings that will take place there, so I think they have become a huge resource for the community for all kinds of things beyond what's on the shelf. — COKIE ROBERTS

cord; it's the creation of the record. It costs a great deal of money to be all over the world gathering news, and somebody's got to pay for that. If people are not buying advertising in newspapers then the newspapers are not going to be able to pay for that and the record will not be complete because we won't know what's going on everywhere, and that is a terrible problem that we're all trying to figure out how to deal with, both the newspapers and broadcast media. Until we find a way to get a financial stream going for the information that people receive on the internet, it's going to be very difficult to keep the actual gathering of the record going."

She added, "A lot of people think, 'well I don't depend on the mainstream media, no, I go to the blogs' or whatever. Well the blogs depend on the mainstream media. Now, you've got to actually get the information from someplace before you start commenting on it, that's all."

There is a strong connection between librarians and journalists, I suggested; that is, journalists create a record of what happens and librarians preserve and disseminate that record. I asked Roberts if she saw that connection.

"Absolutely!" she said. "It's kind of interwoven. As you say, it's journalists finding out what's going on and librarians preserving it and making it available, but also journalists depend on libraries and librarians for information and facts. I mean, the library of today might be in your cell phone instead of going to the building itself, but we need the people who are in the building to get it to the cell phones. It's just the delivery system that's different. But the people actually doing the work and the research are still in libraries."

At the time of the interview, librarian Laura Bush, one of the women Roberts profiles in *We Are Our Mothers' Daughters,* was also First Lady. I asked Roberts how she thought Mrs. Bush was handling her dual roles.

Roberts quipped, "I think if you woke her up in the middle of the night and tickled her and said 'What are you?' she'd say 'a librarian.' But she also found in the White House that there were a lot of other roles that opened up to her, and she became a really energetic and effective fighter for human rights, particularly women's rights, around the world. It's funny because people think of her much more as kind of the 'little lady at home,' but she's the only First Lady ever to go to the White House press room and take the microphone herself. And, when she did, it was to call for the overthrow of the Burmese regime."

How like a librarian, I thought. Besides the atrocities committed by Myanmar's military government, the junta severely restricted internet access, blocking foreign news sites.

The crisis in the American economy was beginning to trickle down to libraries at the time I interviewed Roberts, so I asked her what she thought nonprofits and philanthropic organizations of all kinds should do to make it through the recession in one piece.

"Well, if I had the answer to that I would be making a whole lot of money," she said laughing, "and making it available to other people. But I think that all anybody can do is help it end sooner rather than later and be sensible in terms of what you spend and what you commit to in this period of time. On the other hand, you can't just eviscerate your institution either because that's not a long-haul answer. No, people just have to be very careful and look for as many sources of revenue as they can possibly find."

Part of what libraries are doing is trying to demonstrate their worth and come across as part of the solution to this crisis, I noted.

"In what way?" she asked.

People are going to libraries to look for jobs and learn new skills, I said, and for entertainment and knowledge and information that's free, instead of running out and paying for it.

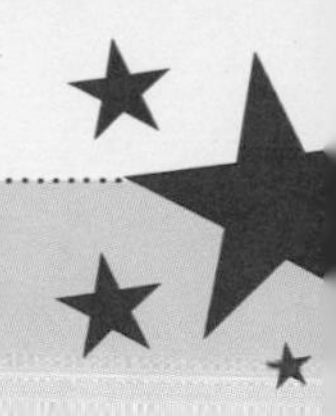

I want my librarians to try to do their very best to stand up to the people who are generally posturing for political reasons when they start talking about banning books in libraries. — COKIE ROBERTS

"That's a very good point," she replied. "If libraries can get that message out, that's a very useful one. It's also useful that libraries have become community institutions, community gathering places. I have been really amazed and heartened by how well—at least to the naked eye—libraries seem to be doing, given the whole age of the internet. I mean anytime I walk into a library it is lively and full of people and lots of kids and there are all kinds of notices tacked up to the bulletin board, there are community gatherings that will take place there, so I think they have become a huge resource for the community for all kinds of things beyond what's on the shelf."

When we talk about libraries we tend to think of public libraries, but I told her we have a lot of surveys and studies that show that children who attend schools with well-stocked and well-staffed school library media centers are higher achievers than those who don't.

"That doesn't surprise me a bit. We know that children's success rates, as studies for decades now have shown, that children who do well in school, it's directly tied to the number of books their parents have in the home," Roberts said, "and I am sure the same thing is true about the number of books in the school. I work a lot with Save the Children, and one of the programs we have going in this country is a literacy program where we not only work hard with the children who are having trouble like trouble reading, but we also stock the libraries because it's terribly important to do so.

"That's the main thing Mrs. Bush has done through the Laura Bush Foundation, but particularly in the Hurricane Katrina–ravaged area she has managed to stock entire children's libraries because she understands how terribly important that is."

I noted that it's been very difficult for the American Library Association to lobby for this at the state level because a lot of times the school library is the first thing to be cut. I asked what she thought was the best way to convey that fundamental piece of information to the public.

"I think the way you have to do that is through the business community," she said. "One of the things that I have learned over the last few years is that the business community has come to understand that if American children are not better educated, they are not going to be competitive. And thank God they've come to understand, because it's so essential for them to do so. Start working with those people and show them good, solid data to corroborate what you're talking about because I think that's

READ MORE

Written by Cokie Roberts

- ★ *Founding Mothers: The Women Who Raised Our Nation*
- ★ *From This Day Forward* (with Steve Roberts)
- ★ *Ladies of Liberty: The Women Who Shaped Our Nation*
- ★ *We Are Our Mothers' Daughters*

the way you start to get the state legislatures involved. It's not just public libraries and it's not just school libraries, it's all kinds of institutions like university libraries or the libraries that are part of historical societies or of historic homes or, of course, the wonderful private libraries like the Huntington. All these places are just incredible resources that we need to nurture and promote because without them we would just not have any direct knowledge, a sense of our history, or a sense of our future, which we can only have some real understanding of if we do have a good grasp of the past."

"What do you want your librarians to do to protect the freedom to read?" I asked.

"I want my librarians to try to do their very best to stand up to the people who are generally posturing for political reasons when they start talking about banning books in libraries. I understand that can be politically difficult for the librarians who are dependent on state funding and dependent on the goodwill of the public. I don't want my librarians to commit suicide in this mission, but I do want them to do the best they can."

I asked Roberts to recall a library moment, that is, a time when a library or a librarian made a significant difference in her life (or at least her day), or with her children or her grandchildren.

"There are so many of them," she said. "I mean I've now written two extensive history books where I spent a huge amount of time in libraries, with librarians suggesting things and finding things. At the Huntington Library in California, which is a fabulous place, they suggested to me the papers—and I would have never known about them—of a woman named Elizabeth Barlow, who was the wife of the American ambassador to France at the time leading up to the War of 1812. Their correspondence was quite fabulous, and in this batch of letters I found all of the invitations that they had received from Napoleon's court. I mean, it was just a fabulous library moment, you know, just seeing them; it was beautiful reading them. And it was all I could do not to just leap and just scare the hell out of my fellow researchers," she laughed.

"But I also have wonderful moments with the children, my grandchildren at this point, when we go to the library and they find something that they're excited about, and what I love is that they can lead you to sections of the library. My twin grandsons, who are seven, who live nearby, they say, 'Come on, Cokie, come over here; here's where the biographies are,' you know. So that's great. But I will tell you my first big library moment was when I was five and I went to the public library in my hometown of New Orleans and went to get a library card and they told me I couldn't because I had to be six or something. And so I did protest and so then there was an agreement that if I could sign my name I could have a card. And I did my whole name, my real name, which is Corinne, so it's longer, but I did my name and I got my library card, and that was great.

"One of the things that I should say is that I've had wonderful experiences just calling up libraries, including the Library of Congress, and asking questions and getting the answers. And that's the other thing that I would encourage everyone to understand: These are living, breathing places with living, breathing people who can help you through a difficult set of questions or a search. They can direct you in ways that Mr. Google cannot, and I think that is a very useful thing for people who are writing, either in school or in grown-up life.

"Librarians should rejoice in the great tradition out of which they come, dating back at least to Alexander, if not before, and the wonderful, wonderful places that they've made in the world and in the country, places where people can find not only wonderful things to read but a sense of belonging and comfort. When you say the word 'library,' it conveys a sense of a place, a good place, a place with meaning, and I think that is a wonderful tradition to be part of." ★

RON REAGAN

political pundit and media host

9

ALONG PARTY LINES

"I grew up in a house where both my parents always had a book on the nightstand."

Ron Reagan is the outspoken son of the late president Ronald Reagan and First Lady Nancy Reagan. A political pundit and analyst, he co-hosted *Connected: Coast to Coast* in 2005 on MSNBC and in 2007 hosted a talk show on KIRO radio in Seattle. He has been a frequent guest on *Larry King Live* on CNN and on Air America Radio. He has also worked as a magazine journalist. He serves on the advisory board of the Creative Coalition, an organization founded in 1989 by a group that included Susan Sarandon and the late Christopher Reeve to politically mobilize entertainers and artists for First Amendment rights, arts advocacy, and public education.

I interviewed Reagan by telephone some weeks before his keynote address at the American Library Association's Annual Conference in June 2008 in Anaheim, where I met him at the convention center. He greeted me warmly, as if he were meeting an old buddy, and then we chatted briefly before his speech.

Photo by Curtis Compton for the American Library Association.

A harsh critic of the Bush administration and the war in Iraq, Reagan was easy to get started. I simply asked him how he thought civil liberties and First Amendment rights were faring in our country these days and what librarians should do in reaction to laws that threaten civil liberties the way portions of the USA Patriot Act did.

"I would like them to do what they have done: Refuse to comply with a law like that, even at the risk of going to prison. I think civil disobedience in a case like this is really what's required. If the FBI or the anti-terror forces, the Office of Homeland Security or whatever, come to a library and say, we want the records of so-and-so, librarians should stand up and simply say no, you don't get them, and I'll burn them before I give them to you."

Reagan said that when he spoke to then American Library Association president Loriene Roy, one of the first things he did was ask her to remind him what the association's stance on First Amendment issues was. "I thought I knew, but I wanted to hear it from her own mouth," he said, "and she told me what I sus-

I think civil disobedience in a case like this is really what's required. If the FBI or the anti-terror forces, the Office of Homeland Security or whatever, come to a library and say, we want the records of so-and-so, librarians should stand up and simply say no, you don't get them. —RON REAGAN

pected, which is you have stood up to the administration's efforts to intrude on people's privacy—for instance, investigators checking people's library records.

"For the last seven years or so, a lot of things have been going on in Washington that aren't business as usual," he said, "and intrusion into our liberties and civil rights is certainly one of those things.

"This election is going to be very significant. We all have a chance to make history here. In fact, we always do every four years. We give somebody the chance to directly make history whether it's Mr. McCain or Mr. Obama in this case. But *we* do that. We are the ones who are making history here, and this is very important because what has been going on for the last seven, eight years in Washington with our government is unprecedented in many ways.

"I don't think that most people fully comprehend, or maybe they don't want to comprehend, really, how far off the rails things have gone, not just with issues of privacy and civil liberties and issues that directly involve the library, but things like torturing and habeas corpus. These concerns have been part of the American psyche for a long time. George Washington refused to torture during the Revolutionary War. It has never been American policy, whatever aberrations might have occurred at various times. It has never been American policy to torture anybody, ever. And now it is.

"A story from an op-ed in the *New York Times* has stayed with me. Following the Iranian hostage crisis back in the 1980s, when the hostages were being released, one of them was a CIA officer who had been tortured by the Iranians. The Iranian officer who had tortured him and interrogated him brought him into his office, sat him down, and apologized to him. He said, 'Look, this ran counter to everything I believe in and my religious beliefs, and I want to make it up to you.' And he said essentially, 'I'll let you do to me what I did to you. I'll give you a free shot basically.' And the CIA officer looked him in the eye and said, 'We don't do that kind of stuff.' Well Americans can't look anybody in the eye anymore and say *we don't do that kind of stuff* because we *do* do that kind of stuff now, and that should be a source of immense shame to us.

One chilling aspect of the 2008 Supreme Court ruling on prisoners at Guantanamo, Reagan said, is that it was only a 5-to-4 ruling. "It should have been a unanimous ruling; there is no way that the Supreme Court of the United States should deny habeas corpus to anyone who's being held by U.S. officials or representatives, and yet four Supreme Court justices—and there was no secret about which four those were going to be—decided to vote to deny it.

"I don't have to tell you this is something that's been canon for centuries now. And to bring up the sort of irrelevant points that they did in their defending opinions . . . Scalia beginning his dissent with the notion that we're at war with radical Islam! So what? What's your point, Mr. Scalia? Or Roberts with his remark that Americans will die as a result of this ruling. Well what's your point, Mr. Roberts? What legal point are you making there? And the almost—I struggle to find a word for it when you apply this to the chief justice of the Supreme Court—the really silly notion, the silly point that he made that if some of these people are released they may well commit other crimes or commit other acts of terror. Well I'm sure, Mr. Roberts, when certain criminals are released from prison some of them go out and commit crimes. Does that mean we should strip habeas corpus from anybody who is accused of a crime? I mean, really, some of the nonsensical things that were coming out of those defending opinions were just striking."

A lot of it had to do with a time-of-war rationale, I suggested, and now that this war has lasted longer than the Second World

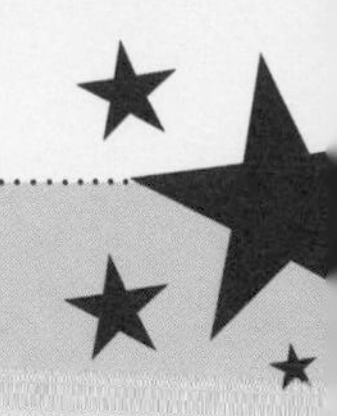

I lobbied to get the librarian to allow me to go into the older section. I remember checking out *One Day in the Life of Ivan Denisovich*—in 6th grade. The quizzical looks the librarian was giving me! But I read it. I can't say I appreciated it the way I should have, but I found it fascinating. —RON REAGAN

War, even people who once supported the Iraq war are questioning it. But he would have none of it, and I tried to move him away from politics and on to more personal topics.

"What role did reading play in your life as you were growing up?" I asked.

"My family has always been a family of readers. I grew up in a house where both my parents always had a book on the nightstand, so I grew up appreciating the pleasure that one got from reading. My mother's biggest problem with me as a little kid was the flashlight under the covers. Trying to get me to actually put the book down and go to bed was a difficult chore."

And the role of libraries when you were a student?

"You probably know that I don't have a stellar academic career," quipped Reagan. "I have a high school diploma. I left college after one semester to become a ballet dancer, so I don't have a college library history behind me.

"I would visit my school library when I was in grade school and high school. I remember being a 6th-grader in a new elementary school—so new that the library was in one of those trailer things, and part of the trailer was roped off and those books were meant only for the older kids—not because they were *Lolita* or anything—but I took exception to this. So I lobbied to get the librarian to allow me to go into the older section. I remember checking out *One Day in the Life of Ivan Denisovich*—in 6th grade. The quizzical looks the librarian was giving me! But I read it. I can't say I appreciated it the way I should have, but I found it fascinating."

Asked for his thoughts on how technology and the internet were affecting education and learning, Reagan said, "Clearly, technology is a help for people like me who need access to information quickly. Google and other tools on the internet are useful; there's no question about that. And obviously it's a useful tool for communication too. I do sometimes wonder, though, whether the surfeit of information that we have is interfering with our ability to actually digest the information. It's not just the amount of information that's important, it's the context of that information and the ability and the time to actually sit and think and digest. I don't think we have a shortage of information by any means in our society, but I think we do run short on the time and the opportunity to really digest and consider that information and arrive at sensible conclusions about that information.

"It's one thing to come up with a list of facts; it's another thing to know the context of those facts and to be able to arrange them in a meaningful way. That's something that many kids have a hard time with. A lot of kids, and a lot of parents too, don't read anymore. Skimming through the internet is not reading; it's simply looking for bullet points. People who don't read deprive themselves of cultivating a habit that I think is useful under any circumstance.

"It's one thing to simply look for some factoid on the internet or anywhere. But reading a book, immersing yourself in another world, sinking into that alternate reality is a very different experience that, if you miss as a kid, is detrimental and very difficult to pick up as an adult. I think it's a little like learning a foreign language; if you don't do it as a kid, it's tougher to pick it up once you get out in the workaday world. If you don't have the knack for it, it's difficult."

I told Reagan that I thought one of the most important things librarians would be interested in was his work with the Creative Coalition and First Amendment rights. He said that he had not worked closely with the Creative Coalition in several years. He explained, "It is dedicated to defending First Amendment rights, among other things. It also is very involved in promoting arts education, the idea being that academics suffer in the absence of a rigorous, complete arts education. That's backed up by scientific studies, particularly involving music education. Music and math, of course, go together, and academic scores improve when there are vital, vibrant music programs available to the students. I've been with the Creative Coalition off and on for about 15 years. I usually go back to Washington and lobby members of Congress, bring a few celebrities along, that always helps."

READ MORE

Recommended by RON REAGAN

- ***Lee and Grant,*** by Gene Smith
- ***Lolita,*** by Vladimir Nabokov
- ***One Day in the Life of Ivan Denisovich,*** by Alexander Solzhenitsyn
- ***Spoon River Anthology,*** by Edgar Lee Masters
- ***The Arabian Nights: Tales from a Thousand and One Nights***

Then I asked Reagan how being the son of a president has affected his professional life and his choices with regard to what he cares about in education, reading, lifelong learning, and how his early life affected those choices.

"Well, boy, that's a good question," he replied. "Since my father was a well-known celebrity—the governor of California when I was eight and then of course on to president—I don't really have anything to compare it with. It's not like we had a normal life until I was 16 and then he became president and everything changed. So it's a little hard to say how it's affected me. I never think of myself being my father's son. I don't walk around daily thinking like that. Other people do, of course, and I daresay that I probably wouldn't have been invited to speak to your association if I hadn't been my father's son. I'm sure I've gotten many professional opportunities because I was my father's son. I've been conscious of the fact that many people have given me opportunities assuming that I probably wouldn't be very good at what they were asking me to do, but that my name value would make up for that, and I've been pleased to say generally they're surprised that I'm actually pretty good at what I do." He laughed and added, "I don't choose to do things that I don't think I can do a good job at."

"As far as education and becoming a reader and a sort of bookish person, again, that didn't have much to do with my father's position in life as governor or president or anything else. It

READ MORE

Written by Ron Reagan

★ *My Father at 100*

had more to do with the fact that my parents just read. I mean there were books around all the time. My father, when he was a younger man, signed up with the Book-of-the-Month Club, their special leather-bound edition," he laughed. "So he had not an extensive but a pretty impressive small library of leather-bound editions of classic literature. When I was growing up I used it, spent a lot of time in our den where the books were kept, for the most part, and just going through all these books. I was too young to really appreciate or understand—I mean when you're 10, 12 years old you're probably not going to get all that much out of *Lee and Grant,* but you're reading it nevertheless. The words are sinking in, the rhythms are sinking in, and the images are making an impression on you. *Spoon River Anthology, A Thousand and One Nights*—all these books were there all the time and you could always just walk into that den, that little library, and pull a book off the shelf and go somewhere to sit and read it."

I couldn't resist turning the topic back to the current White House, wondering what Reagan thought of Laura Bush. I noted that while the president's ratings were at an all-time low, hers were up.

"Well, people don't generally dump on all first ladies—unless they're Hillary Clinton, of course."

Eleanor Roosevelt was beloved and despised, I reminded him.

"Well that's true," he said. "My mother took some shots too and some of them were about being 'plastic.' They said Bess Truman was frumpy."

Reagan concluded that it's hard to hold the first lady actually responsible for what the administration is doing because she's not really responsible. ★

GARRISON KEILLOR

radio personality, writer, humorist

10

THE INTERNET IS A SWAMP

"I still go into the enormous reading rooms of the New York Public Library, cathedrals of literature and of reading, of study, of ambition, of the whole entrepreneurial spirit."

The library "is where like-minded people go to encourage each other and do it silently," said Garrison Keillor. "To me this is almost miraculous." The author of more than a dozen books and the creator, host, and writer of *A Prairie Home Companion* on public radio, Keillor talked with me after his June 26 speech at the American Library Association's Annual Conference in Washington, D.C., in 2007, sharing his views on the traditional role of libraries in a technological age. His new novel, *Pontoon*, was being published that month.

The interview with the 64-year-old curmudgeon was a difficult one. I was scheduled between his book signing and his train home from Washington, but he stayed too long in the exhibit

Photo by Andrew Harrer for Bloomberg, courtesy of Getty Images.

hall, and the only thing his manager could offer was the 10-minute walk back to his hotel.

I waited for him with my Flip video camera ready to go. After an introduction, I asked if I could get a comment about the conference, and I aimed the camera at him. He looked straight into the lens like a bulldog and started growling.

A little discombobulated, I followed him like a puppy from the convention center to his hotel, holding my tape recorder up to his face while traffic zoomed all around us, making much of what he said inaudible.

"You've said that libraries are the best counterterrorism tool we have," I said.

"That was a joke," he replied, straight-faced.

I told him that I had laughed at the line but still wanted to know if in some sense there wasn't an element of truth in the statement.

"In the sense that people who are devout readers are unlikely to commit violent acts against strangers," Keillor agreed. But he went on to say, "Libraries are struggling for a rationale. Everybody I know is trying to grab onto this strange world that we live in, but there's so much residual loyalty to libraries. It must run

When you walk into a library, you see all these strangers . . . engaged in ambitious projects. They have no idea what the outcome will be. They are taking big risks. There's courage there, and I value that. — GARRISON KEILLOR

very deep, so I think libraries have some time to find a purpose. I'm pretty sure that we're seeing the death of the newspaper business as we know it, and that throws us into a world that's very strange for people my age. I don't know how democracy works without newspapers. I simply don't."

"Or how it transfers to the Web?" I said.

"It doesn't," he snapped. "But this will simply have to find its own course. I think libraries have enough time to figure this out. To go technical, to get wired up, to be about data retrieval and so on, in one way. But book publishing has a large future. There have been many attempts to try to squeeze the book into electronic media, and I just don't see that happening very soon. As long as book publishing survives, then people, simply by habit, will look to libraries."

"You don't believe that everything is on the internet?" I asked.

"The internet is just an enormous, interesting swamp. It's full of self-promotion, it's full of bad information, and it's full of everything. And you can sort of maneuver your way around it, from island to island, and you can find things of interest, but I think there still is room for paper between covers. People have a limited amount of time, and if you take a hard look at the amount of time you can spend drifting, trying to get your bearings on the internet, you are grateful for people who can save you time and that's what librarians do—they save you enormous amounts of time."

"You seem to value a lot of traditional aspects of what makes a library," I observed.

"I still go into the enormous reading rooms of the New York Public Library, cathedrals of literature and of reading, of study, of ambition, of the whole entrepreneurial spirit. I walk down those long rows of library tables and library lamps—but now with outlets for laptops—and it's a place where you are in the midst of other people who are ambitious, too.

"If you're trying to write a book or a paper or anything, you have these big mood swings and ups and downs. When you walk into a library, you see all these strangers—each one with his or her own little nest of notes and books—engaged in ambitious projects. They have no idea what the outcome will be. They are taking big risks. There's courage there, and I value that."

"And what about chatting with these kindred spirits?" I asked.

"We never talk, ever. You walk into a library of the sort I'm talking about or the St. Paul Public Library in Minnesota, and there is zero schmoozing. Same as when I was up at the university. If people went in there for a good time and to laugh and joke and whisper and gossip, they were shushed by other people. This is something that nobody will ever express in a mission statement. It'll never be expressed in the goals and objectives.

READ MORE

written by Garrison Keillor

- *The Book of Guys: Stories*
- *A Christmas Blizzard*
- *Happy to Be Here*
- *Homegrown Democrat: A Few Plain Thoughts from the Heart of America*
- *Lake Wobegon Days*
- *Leaving Home*
- *Liberty: A Novel of Lake Wobegon*
- *Life among the Lutherans*
- *Pilgrims: A Lake Wobegon Romance*
- *Pontoon: A Novel of Lake Wobegon*
- *77 Love Sonnets*
- *Wobegon Boy*

Management is never going to have a meeting about this. Nonetheless, to me it's the most basic thing that's true of libraries."

Although he was sounding like a Luddite, he mentioned that he was facing a column deadline and that he would be filing the column online on the train, enabled by technology. I noted that technology has changed his life in ways similar to the way it has changed libraries.

"Yeah, yeah," he said. "I know. Oh, it's made a huge difference. It's made work portable. It all changed when we went from the electric typewriter to a portable computer. And it made everything so much better."

He noted that he could work on his material right on up to the moment of broadcast. "We never could do that before, you know, and it just cut out the whole laborious process of typing and typing and retyping and retyping. So it was a huge thing," he admitted.

At the end of the interview, I stood dripping from our fast-paced walk and the heat in his hotel lobby and thanked Keillor for talking with me. He suddenly softened, grabbed my hand, looked me right in the eye for the first time, and said, "You're a good man." And he was off. ★

RALPH NADER

consumer advocate, author, political activist

11

RALLYING READERS

"Books in our household were both generally revered and specifically dissected."

The cash-strapped District of Columbia Public Library, whose sorry state was documented during 2002 in the *Washington Post,* found a champion in Ralph Nader. The consumer activist and former presidential candidate hosted a $10,000-a-table benefit dinner at the Carnegie Institution December 11, to rally philanthropists and business leaders around the library.

"If I don't do it, no one is going to do it," Nader said, lamenting the abysmal state of support for the library. Less than 0.7% of the city's budget goes to DCPL, he observed, noting that the system had 200 more staff members in 1976 than it had 27 years later. The initial goal of Nader's campaign was to raise $350,000 for an 18-month improvement blitz that would include tax dollars for long overdue repairs to the system's 27 branches.

Nader also wanted to gain long-term political and community support for boosting the library's budget and for new activities focusing on children, the arts, and literacy. A man of little personal wealth, Nader said he hoped to do for the District of

Photo by Lois Raimondo for the Washington Post, courtesy of Getty Images.

Columbia Public Library what Vartan Gregorian had done for the New York Public Library. Now president of Carnegie Corporation of New York, Gregorian, as NYPL president from 1981 to 1989, was able to turn that library's funding situation around by making it chic to be a library supporter.

Nader said he also wanted to give the library a voice in D.C. government. "Somebody of his stature will open doors for us," then District of Columbia library director Molly Raphael told me at the time. She said the project was "a tremendous opportunity" that Nader proposed to her after reading about the library's plight last summer. She said he sent 250 new gift books and asked that they be spread around the system, and then called two days later and began formulating his plan.

A tattered flag atop the District of Columbia's Watha T. Daniel-Shaw branch library may have already found a replacement donor, said Nader, but broken equipment and shabby facilities will require a larger commitment from city leaders. A lifelong library patron and nearly 50-year D.C. resident, Nader said that the library's short hours, inadequate collections, and neglected buildings are unacceptable, but "this is not going to be turned around on the inside; it needs external force, from the neighborhoods to the glitterati."

Raphael agreed that "every line in the budget is underfunded." She said that 30 years ago the percentage of the D.C. budget that supported the library was 1.2%; now, "even 1% would make all the difference." She said she saw two aspects to the campaign:

I really don't need another cause, but reading about the state of libraries made me blush with shame. —RALPH NADER

mobilizing the community to push the city and seeking private sector and foundation support. Nader retained Kike Arnal to produce a gripping photography exhibit for the kick-off dinner; the display featured bleak black-and-white photos of the system's deteriorating facilities, contrasted with color photos of successful big-city library revitalization projects in other parts of the country to show the 80 or so attendees "what we could be."

Nader, who is director of the Center for the Study of Responsive Law, was particularly disturbed by one photo of "a reading room at a branch taken through a window with a bullet hole that has been there for two years." Other photos showed out-of-order signs, peeling paint, cracked walls, torn carpets, and outdated materials. "I really don't need another cause," Nader said, "but reading about the state of libraries made me blush with shame. In the middle of this real-estate boom, we have private affluence and public squalor."

When I interviewed Nader about his library advocacy for the first time, I convinced him to write an opinion piece for *American Libraries* titled "A Renaissance in Washington." Published in the March 2003 issue, here's what he wrote.

READING THE MAY 30, 2002, *Washington Post,* I came upon a long article by Judith Havemann on the deprived, decaying, and disrespected state of the Washington, D.C., library system. The main Martin Luther King Jr. Library and its 26 branches, the article reported, have suffered budget and staff reductions that stand in marked contrast with the office-building boom and the expansion of multimillionaires in our federal district.

I read on to learn that from the mid-'70s to now, staff has been cut by 30% to 432 and the library's share of the city's budget has been reduced from 1.6% to 0.7%. The result is devastating. As *Post* columnist Marc Fisher described: "Open six evenings a week in the 1970s, branches now stay open only two evenings. No branch is open on Sundays. Roofs leak, walls sag, shelves are a mess. Collections are insultingly out of date and incomplete." And, of course, usage has declined.

A little over two weeks later, I called Havemann to say that such a graphic article must have sparked a wave of calls and expressions of support. She replied that she had received a few calls, but nothing like a wave.

I was stunned, though I should not have been. Washington is a city of two layers (local and federal) straddling three jurisdictions (the District of Columbia, Virginia, and Maryland). It is a city tensed between private affluence and public squalor. The poverty has to be seen to be believed, which is why tourists are guided away from the desolate and devastating areas of our national capital.

But libraries? They should be an easy cause, a ready commitment, an obvious mission for philanthropists and movers and shakers among the well-to-do. After all, weren't libraries in comparable need turned around in New York City, Boston, Cleveland, Denver, and San Francisco by a combination of civic leadership and noblesse oblige?

I called Vartan Gregorian, who in the '80s rescued the giant New York Public Library system with the help of Brooke Astor and her coterie of affluent New Yorkers. Gregorian was quite familiar with the D.C. situation, having given the library a $500,000 grant. With typical elation, he offered advice on how it was done in New York and mentioned an address he delivered in St. Louis where he called community support for public libraries "an investment in the educational, cultural, economic, and civic life of the city that multiplies itself once it reaches critical mass." Clearly, a form of urban renewal writ large.

The plight of the D.C. library system reflects the disintegration of community here. How could the city's power structure sit

But libraries? They should be an easy cause, a ready commitment, an obvious mission for philanthropists and movers and shakers among the well-to-do. —RALPH NADER

idly by and watch tens of thousands of youngsters grow up without a library experience? The same way that it avoids rolling up its sleeves to provide decent education for those same youngsters. The same way it can look indifferently on statistics showing that one-third of district adults are functionally illiterate. It is enough to make us all blush with shame.

Our forebears had more pride. Even in the Great Depression of the '30s, very few libraries or branches closed down. Now after the biggest macro boom in our history, libraries and librarians have to go around with a tin cup!

I don't need another cause but this one could not be avoided. Our Center for the Study of Responsive Law has launched a D.C. Library Renaissance Project with a dinner at the Carnegie Institution building attended by many of the district's leading citizens, including Donald Graham, publisher of the *Washington Post*, who made an impassioned plea for revitalizing these libraries. At the dinner, startling photographs by Enrique Arnal of the dilapidated condition of the libraries visually demonstrated the challenges.

The first note of optimism came from the D.C. librarians and Friends of the Library at the dinner. Instead of being defensive, they welcomed this pictorial reality that placed grimness before those guests who lived in the "other Washington" and were not patrons of the library's services. Library director Molly Raphael knows that realizing the abysmal neglect provides the necessary umph or jolt to motivate improvements.

Everyone in the D.C. government, from the mayor on down, says the right things and points to the mayor's vision statements emphasizing the role that a resurgent library can play in adult education and literacy programs. At the same time, district officials are letting literacy and basic adult education programs for the city's neediest residents disappear. Over the years, there has been more talk and less action for the libraries.

Enter the Renaissance Project to mobilize support, from the neighborhoods to the glitterati; from the frustrated supporters of the branches to the lawyers, the businesspersons, and the professionals who get their calls returned; from the absence of the cultural and civic events to the presence of more of Washington's authors, musicians, artists, poets, and civic leaders lending their talents; from the massive deferred maintenance to the renovations and expansion of facilities; from the pitiful philanthropy to a plentiful philanthropy.

This is a tall order only because of the deep-seated anomie that afflicts too many influential people toward their community. But as Gregorian counseled, no matter how much private support they receive, public libraries are a public responsibility of the municipal government first and foremost. Which is another way of defining community.

The next time I spoke with Nader was in 2007. He called me out of the blue to say that he'd been thinking about the American Library Association and had written a piece that he thought I might like to publish. I did, in the November issue of American Libraries. *We called it "From a Land of Books," in which "the son of Lebanese immigrants looks back at the way his parents infused their children with a critical love for the written word." In his own words:*

IT WOULD BE AN OVERSTATEMENT to say that my parents' four children grew up in a home of wall-to-wall books. There were bookcases in the living room, the pantry, and all the bedrooms, but not the kitchen and dining room, where their contents were regularly discussed and debated. Clearly, we relished books—nonfiction, fiction, encyclopedias, poetry, and, for my sisters, books about music.

We were so steeped in books that we regularly filled our maximum quota of borrowing three books at a time from the Beardsley and Memorial Library, which was just a stroll away. The library was our sanctuary for insatiable curiosity, providing us with inviting open stacks, literally grottoes of mystery and wonder.

We were not immune from boasting in front of our parents about how many books we were reading each week. They would have none of that. "Reading is just page turning," my mother would say, "unless you understand, digest, and remember what you're reading." "Imagine what a bargain books are for readers," my father once observed. "The author spends months or years writing the book. You reap the benefits of that effort in just a few hours."

During my teen years, I read the legendary American muckrakers—Ida Tarbell, Lincoln Steffens, Upton Sinclair, George Seldes, and Ferdinand Lundberg—while trembling with excitement as they documented and excoriated major corporate injustices of their era. I would run to the library to return books so I could borrow more of the works we somehow never found part of our classroom studies. What a supplement the library was to my schooling.

Both my parents steered us toward learning about the history of our little hometown, Winsted, Connecticut (population 10,000), from its natural surroundings to its many factories and

READ MORE
Recommended by RALPH NADER

★ The books of Ida Tarbell, Lincoln Steffens, Upton Sinclair, George Seldes, and Ferdinand Lundberg

philanthropies. Reading about the local charities, I learned that Ellen Rockwell Beardsley started our town's library with a $10,000 donation at the turn of the 20th century. I thought how pleased she would have been to see how intensively her gift to the community has been used.

We used to say that we were instructed in school but educated at home and at the library.

To be sure, books in our household were both generally revered and specifically dissected. One day my older brother, Shafeek, brought home a brand-new set of the *Encyclopedia Americana*. It was the 1947 edition. Having just returned from the Navy and World War II, he wanted his younger siblings to embrace a wider frame of the world and its knowledge. After placing the many volumes neatly on a shelf, he called me over and began reading to me a passage from the entry of Hawaii. The reader was informed that the reigning Queen Liliuokalani was deposed in 1893, a republic was formed, and "pursuant to the request of the people of Hawaii, as expressed through the legislation of the republic . . . the islands were formally annexed to the United States on August 12, 1898, as a territory."

Shaf looked up at me when he finished reading. "Do you know what really happened? The wealthy white planters and some missionaries engineered a coup to overthrow the native Hawaiian monarchy. This was no request of the people. It was simple colonial imperialism, secured by the U.S. Marines. Here this encyclopedia is whitewashing history." That was a memorable lesson in skepticism. Even an established encyclopedia, I learned, could contain propaganda.

My father provided more than one occasion to sharpen our inquiring minds. He would always chuckle when he saw books, teachers, and townspeople speak of Columbus discovering America, asking, "Didn't the people who greeted him on the shores arrive before he did?"

My parents had one tradition that consciously rejected books. When we were little and being tucked into our beds, Mother would tell us children's stories from her fertile memory, stories she'd learned in the oral tradition growing up in Lebanon. She would not read to us, because she wanted to look into our eyes and uninterruptedly take in our wondrous expressions. A book would only have intruded into such personal moments.

Years later, during a visit to Lebanon in the early sixties, I purchased and shipped back to my father about 400 books of history, fiction, and the literary arts, in Arabic. He devoured them in about 20 months, in between long days at his sprawling family restaurant—a town talkfest on Main Street, opposite the textile mills.

There was one book I was not able to share with my mother and father: my love story for them, my book, *The Seventeen Traditions*, about the ways they reared four children in the 1930s, '40s, and '50s, about how they conveyed a critical love of books and what they had to teach us. My parents helped spark the weave of learning and experiencing that melded family values with civic improvement values and business values into that overall intangible mix of knowledge and engagement.

They were proverbial parents, using proverbs for our enlightenment and discipline. But one proverb from ancient China that they did not convey embraced their philosophy of books concisely: "To know and not to do is not to know."

At the 2003 American Library Association Annual Conference in Toronto, Nader was the closing speaker. "Commercialism diminishes everyone," he said, noting that television is 90% advertising and tawdry entertainment. "The public airways do not belong to the public," the consumer activist told a capacity crowd in the 1,300-seat convention center auditorium.

"Try to get a library story on the evening news," Nader challenged. Library budgets have to become "power budgets" by rallying public support, he said, observing that many American public and school libraries face budget cuts of 15% or more. And don't plead in "that forlorn tone of a beleaguered librarian," he urged.

Nader's speech moved quickly to national politics. "When the Bushes and the Cheneys talk about the most powerful country in the world, they are talking about military power, not humanitarian power, certainly not library power."

The financial plight of libraries is part of a broader attack on community, Nader said, and comes at a time when half of the U.S. government's discretionary expenditures will be military. He denounced the "corporate crime wave," the commercialization of our society, and the "corporate takeover of budget priorities" in the public sector.

READ MORE

written by RALPH NADER

- *Civic Arousal*
- *Crashing the Party: Taking on the Corporate Government in an Age of Surrender*
- *Cutting Corporate Welfare*
- *The Good Fight: Declare Your Independence and Close the Democracy Gap*
- *In Pursuit of Justice: Collected Writings 2000–2003*
- *No Contest: Corporate Lawyers and the Perversion of Justice in America* (with Wesley J. Smith)
- *"Only the Super-Rich Can Save Us!"*
- *The Ralph Nader Reader*
- *The Seventeen Traditions*
- *Unsafe at Any Speed: The Designed-In Dangers of the American Automobile*

"Corporate welfare towers over poverty welfare," Nader said, demanding to know how President Bush was going to spend the $26,000 he'll receive from his own tax cut. "He ought to give the money to the District of Columbia Public Library. That would make Laura Bush happy." He then noted that he believed Mrs. Bush has helped persuade her husband to increase federal funding for libraries from $112 million to $285 million, but much of this money is earmarked for training new librarians, "who are going to find themselves looking for jobs in crumbling libraries or looking for jobs that aren't there."

And if a library system is on the upswing? It's because there are "enough people in the community who say it's going to be done," Nader asserted. Reviving libraries, especially in our cities, represents "educational renewal, civic renewal, and urban renewal, all in one."

He cited the testimony of a 12-year-old girl who, at a public hearing, told the District of Columbia city council that she was grateful for the opportunity to speak before the group because it was the first time she had ever done anything for her country: "She was redefining patriotism: Do something for your country: Read!"

Nader said he was troubled by the misguided notion that libraries have been rendered unnecessary by the internet. "If any of you know of an internet program that has reduced illiteracy, let me know." The great success of technology, he said, is that it has permitted the participation of people with disabilities.

Where libraries are concerned, the great success of Nader's efforts has been to draw attention to the need.

As Molly Raphael once said, "Ralph Nader understands the importance of having adequate public support before significant private resources will be achievable. He also believes that the effort around the D.C. Public Library may serve as a model for how to engage the citizenry in local government, one of the challenges that we in D.C. face more than most other jurisdictions." ★

JAMIE LEE CURTIS

actress, children's author

12

A CONNECTION TO LEARNING

"I don't think you should have to love to read books that are crappy."

Author-actress Jamie Lee Curtis lent her star power to the American Library Association's 2008 Annual Conference in Anaheim with a special media event during which she read her latest book, *Big Words for Little People*, to children from the ALA childcare facility in the convention center. She then keynoted the Public Library Association's President's Program.

I caught up with Curtis for a quick Q&A before she went onstage and asked her why she started writing books for children. "I didn't start writing books because it was a connection to learning. For me, it was a connection to feeling. It spoke to me from a creative standpoint," she said.

Asked when she started thinking of herself as a writer, Curtis said, "I didn't use the words 'writer' or 'author' for a couple of years because I think of myself as a reader, and the import of that

Photo by Andrew Eccles, courtesy of HarperCollins.

title, 'author,' is so monstrous for me that it's taken me a long time to own the fact that I am an author."

"What do you like best about being an author?" I asked. She told me it was "sitting in front of a group of children and having them engage with me—them understanding what I'm talking about, at a level that is eye-to-eye."

Curtis was vivacious and irreverent, very much the sexy and hilarious star of *True Lies* and *A Fish Called Wanda*. Her answers to my questions were all over the map, rambling free association that always somehow managed, nevertheless, to get to the point.

"I enjoyed it," Curtis said of her energetic session reading to the children, which seemed only to have warmed her up for the day's work. While thrilled to be in Anaheim to speak to librarians, she said, the children are "who it's for."

When somebody like her puts her celebrity behind reading and literacy and lifelong learning, I told Curtis, it's important for libraries and meaningful to librarians, whose role in education is sometimes underestimated.

"I don't connect to it from a scholastic side," Curtis warned, laughing, "because the perfect truth is I'm an underachiever academically. I barely got out of high school. I can't spell. I mean, I asked grandma questions all day long. 'Is it me and you or I and you?' 'Is it me and I?' 'I go to the market?' 'You and I go to the market?' I mean, really; I'm a functional illiterate. I can't spell a word. If you ask me to write a paper, I won't be able to write a paper. So I don't approach this from that standpoint.

"What I'm interested in is connecting and relating. And if I can connect and relate to a child, a book, and love of reading comes from it, that's beautiful. But I don't attack it from the reading-gets-you-there view, that reading will bring in the emotion. I go emotion into reading. I would have never written a book from the outside. I had to go into something where it was like I felt something."

What do books give children? What is reading for a child? It's freedom. See, a book is freedom. —JAMIE LEE CURTIS

Curtis reflected on the inspiration for her first book, *When I Was Little: A Four-Year-Old's Memoir of Her Youth.* "My daughter stated ownership; I am four, and I'm here!" Curtis said, explaining that her daughter was essentially saying she was not a baby anymore. "And that made me go, 'hmm, a 4-year-old's memoir of her youth?' and it made me laugh, and find the nugget of some emotional content.

"I am an actor from instinct only. I didn't come to acting from, 'Well, I've studied at Juilliard and I can do 15 accents, and I can break a script down, I can break a scene down, I know character study.' I don't know anything. But if you ask me to play Queen Elizabeth, I'll play Queen Elizabeth. Not because I will do it from the outside in; I'll do it from the inside out. And that's how I am as a writer, it's from the inside out.

"The fact that I'm an author who now promotes the very thing that I didn't do very well as a child is thrilling for me, but it's not from some pastiche of 'you gotta love to read,' because honestly, I don't think you should have to love to read books that are crappy. I don't think you should have to love badly written books. I don't think you should have to love boring books. I think you should have to love terrific books. And that's why Harry Potter blew the roof off of the children's book market, because it was mind-blowing."

Of her book *Big Words for Little People,* Curtis said it was born at BookExpo four years earlier, when she gave a keynote speech in the morning and told the story of a 4-year-old's memoir of her youth. Much of the speech was about "my complete neophyteness, if that's a word," Curtis said. She also told the story of the "only argument" she ever had with her editor, Joanna Cotler, over a line that she had written in the book: "When I was little, I didn't know what consequences were. Now I do, but I don't like them." Cotler thought that a 4-year-old wouldn't know what the word "consequences'" meant and the editors had advised that she replace it with "an age-appropriate word." They went back and forth a little bit, said Curtis, "and I kind of caved." The line was changed to "When I was little, I didn't know what time-outs were. Now, I do, but I don't like them."

Curtis said she and her editor walked back to the exhibit hall debating the change, Cotler feeling a little embarrassed that Curtis had brought up their little disagreement in front of so many people because it looked as if they had had a fight over it. "And so we were walking by the stalls," Curtis explained, "and I said, 'You know, Joanna, we should probably just turn it into a book, *Big Words for Little People.*' Ding, ding, ding, ding, ding. And that's how the book was born."

I asked Curtis to explain more about how reading empowers children in ways that maybe video games and television do not.

"I'm the mother of a 12-year-old boy with learning disabilities," she said. "My son is a multimedia kid. My kid is at computer camp this week, you know. I have a boy for whom the computer is a port from which his creativity and imagination come pouring out, and the imagination offered in the technology draws him deeply. And I don't fight it, because how many guys did I grow up with who were Dungeons & Dragons fans? That's my son. He's that guy. So he's the World of Warcraft, which is a beautiful, fable-like, role-playing game, and you go into these worlds and you have experiences.

"I'm a big proponent of technology, as long as there are limits to it, as long as there's good balance, like a healthy diet. I'm fine with a little of that. I'm fine with some fresh vegetables. We don't have to choose one and exclude all the others, because there is no exclusion, life is not exclusionary. If we did that, honestly and this with all due respect, we'd all be Amish or we'd be an Orthodox Jew, living in a very protected environment where you control the input into your children. But if you're a person who travels the world, there is no control, because you're the control. You're the filter. You can decide what is appropriate and inappropriate." Curtis pointed out that the two words in *Big Words for Little People* that are "the biggest parent words in the book" are "What is *appropriate*? What is *inappropriate*? And why?"

"What do books give children? What is reading for a child? It's freedom. See, a book is freedom. A book is the port into a world, like *The Princess Bride*, for example, or *RuneWarriors*. You open that door, you're in another world. Harry Potter, you open that door, you're in another world. I love the freedom that reading gives you, which is why anybody corralling the ideas with any sort of controls bothers me. Yeah, there's appropriate and inappropriate. I certainly think that there are inappropriate things in certain books that only an older child should be able to read. Should the diary of Anne Frank be a 7-year-old's book or a 5-year-old's book? I don't think so. Are you really exploring the Holocaust for the 5-year-old? But with an 11-year-old? Absolutely, because their understanding of life and death is very different.

"What books give anybody, me, is freedom—freedom to stop being me and freedom to explore another world that I would never get a chance to. And that to me is life and living and all the reasons why we're here—to explore and have the freedom of imagination and the belief that we can, too, write whatever we want."

An article in *AARP* magazine had recently profiled Curtis, calling her "an exuberant crusader for aging wisely" and quoting her as having said, "Getting older means paring yourself down to an essential version of yourself." I asked her how I could pare myself down to an essential version of myself. She went off on a wildly entertaining diatribe about essence.

"It's like essential oil," she said. "Have you ever experimented with any sort of essential oil? Something that has been condensed. It's like reducing something on a stove, and the stronger you reduce it, the more flavor comes out, the more true essence of it comes out. When you really get into that essence, that delicious, deep, aromatic essence of yourself, you're in the zone. You're in that essential you. And it really, for me, is a multistep experience. It has to do with divesting stuff. I'm a big divester of stuff. I don't own more than I need. I look at the world and think, 'Oh, stop this train.' It's just this acquisition, where here in America, we're acquisition maniacs. We have this idea that everything can be on credit and everybody can have everything. And it's just stuff, stuff, stuff, stuff, stuff. And everywhere you look, there's stuff, stuff, stuff, stuff, stuff. And it's almost unpatriotic for you not to buy the stuff, because somehow you're not keeping the machine going.

"I would say hold onto every penny you have right now and ride. Don't go shopping today. Sell your gas guzzler and buy a Prius if you can afford it.

"It has to do with divesting physical stuff, but it also has to do then with divesting people. You look around your day; how many times have you had some contact with some friend that you made 20 years ago that now you can't even remember why you became friends, and you go, Why do I know this person? Every time I see them, they're either in trauma or . . . If this isn't a good relationship, get out. You can say to people, You know what? I wish you well in the world. I really do. You're a good person. But I'm going to move on from this relationship. It's not helping me. It's just not. And I'm sorry to say that and I'm sure that's hurtful for you.' Or just don't call them back!" Curtis laughed.

"A person I admire a lot said to me just recently, 'Aging is God's way of telling you, you don't have time to waste.' And if you try to keep it away, you're denying that reality. And you're giving yourself less and less time to figure out what the F you're doing here. Or why the F you're here. If you're aging, the first time you wake up and go, 'Oh, my back,' you have to realize, if you ever wanted to climb Everest, you better go freaking do it tomorrow. Or if you ever wanted to run a marathon and you're waking up and you're like me today, I was like, 'Ooh, man,' right away. That's God telling me, 'Jamie, you don't have time to waste.' And it's a beautiful thing to remember. That's why we age. We age because if we don't start essentializing and figuring out what are we doing here? What are we going to have been known to our people for? What do we really want to say to the world? In whatever capacity, I don't care what the capacity is. Put a sign up in your store window that says what you believe."

Curtis went on to talk about a stranger who had handed her his business card during the conference. The card read, "Ask

READ MORE

Recommended by JAMIE LEE CURTIS

- ★ ***The Diary of a Young Girl,*** by Anne Frank
- ★ ***RuneWarriors,*** by James Jennewein and Tom S. Parker
- ★ ***The Princess Bride,*** by William Goldman

the question," and Curtis found that to represent another kind of essence. "Put that up in your freaking window of your store or your library," she laughed. "Ask the question. What question? There's the question. What are we doing? What is your life for? Why are you here? Why am I here? And that, to me, then gets into that very question of why we are aging. Because I'm not sure I was thinking that when I was 20. But at 50, I'm thinking it. This is the reason why we age, so that we can realize that we don't have time to spare with people, with ourselves, with anything that we're just so sick and tired of doing. Well, if you're sick and tired of being sick and tired of being sick and tired of being sick and tired, change!"

I interrupted her to announce that I had reached that point.

"Me too," she enthused, "so welcome to the change club! Because without it, we're going to be 80-year-old people saying, 'I have regrets.' I don't want to have regrets. I want to have reality. I want to have courage. I want to be able to look back and say, 'Wow, I saw something and changed who I am.' And that's, to me, really an important, profound statement.

Libraries to me are like great coaches on a team. They are there in support. If you have a baseball team, the teacher's the manager and the head coach, but then there are the batting coaches and the catching coach. That's what libraries offer. They offer this great infrastructure of support.

—JAMIE LEE CURTIS

"Ultimately the fact that I'm here at all is about change and my own personal change. It's about acceptance. It's the kind of classic conversation that we just had, which is looking at your life, looking at the world, and figuring out what you aren't happy with and then making change. And how do we get there from a librarian's standpoint? How do we relate to get more people in, who want to be part of books, who want to be part of a community? How do we do that?"

Curtis had plenty of advice. She recalled walking into the room that had been set up for her to read to and talk with the children at the conference. "You know it's interesting," she said, "I walked into that room today and it was very quiet. And I walked in there and I asked, 'Why is it so quiet?' and someone said, 'It's a library event' and I went 'Oh.' Honestly, and I'm about to say something that's probably blasphemous, but I didn't like going to museums because they felt like prisons to me, until I could move as fast as I wanted to move in a museum. I understand there are inside voices and outside voices, I get it. But it's not a church; it's a room of ideas. And I'm nervous anytime I'm told to button it up, put my mute button on, or sit where I'm not allowed to move or do anything. How am I going to feel a part of it? Now, that's mostly because I didn't go to libraries as a child and when I went it was with a class and it was always the teacher going 'Class! What are the rules of the library? You don't touch! You don't talk!'

"I've not been to the library where they've brought in Nintendo Guitar Hero nights, or having loud Wednesdays where for 10 minutes everybody in the place is allowed to talk as loud as they want. I would encourage shaking it up and saying, 'Attention Library Listeners, for three minutes everyone is going to talk at full voice' and just let people get their ya-yas out. Because if you ask a child to sit here like this, they're children, they can't. If you say to a child, 'All right you've sat there, now everybody get up, do the whacko dance, do some jumping jacks, run in place, stop, run in place, stop, close your eyes, open them, put your hands out, close your eyes, feel the room spin, open your eyes, touch the floor, anything!' And then say 'Sit down.' That, to me, needs to be explored. I'm just telling you from my experience. Anytime something feels like it's just a prison where you're not allowed to move and you're not allowed to do anything, that isn't good, so for me, libraries used to represent this kind of rigidity. And the more I hear when I meet these kind of cool groovy librarians, I'm like, yeah!

"I'm not saying be disrespectful and I understand that some people are studying and they need quiet. But there's room for everybody and I would create ways for children, particularly, to have some space to be children and make that a place that's much more user-friendly. Well, I like the children's reading rooms, but ultimately everything has to change. We can't continue educating our children the way we educate them. It's not working. It's clearly not working.

"You can complain all you want, people can come up with excuses about why it is, but it is. And unless we change it, we're in big trouble. The big word will be *trouble*. And I think that it really needs to be addressed. Clearly the Gates Foundation is going, 'Oh, yeah.' So I'm going to start doing a lot more work with them."

Curtis also pointed with pride to her work with the Children Affected by AIDS Foundation and her role in passing the Children's Hospital Bond in California four years earlier. "We're going to put another bond on the ballot to raise hundreds of millions of dollars to build and support the infrastructure of children's hospitals up and down the state," she said.

Clearly, her work with sick children had affected her view of education and sports.

"Libraries to me are like great coaches on a team. They are there in support. If you have a baseball team, the teacher's the manager and the head coach, but then there are the batting coaches and the catching coach. That's what libraries offer. They offer this great infrastructure of support.

"Any child can walk into a library and say 'I'm doing a report on photosynthesis and I really need some help because I'm struggling with it and my teacher suggested I come to a library.'

"And that librarian will be very happy to help point that child in a direction, go over to that child later and say, 'Hey, how are you doing? What'd you find? Would you like to go in a little deeper?'

"Or the kid who comes in with a summer reading list and says, 'I don't want to read anything.'

"And the librarian might look at the list and go, 'You know *RuneWarriors* is a great book for boys about a Viking.'

'I'm not interested in Vikings.'

'Do you know anything about Vikings?'

'No.'

'Do you know they were great warriors?'

'No.'

'They sailed ships, they wore monstrous shields?'

'No.'

'Would you be interested in seeing a picture of a Viking?'

'Sure.'

"Get a book on Vikings, and then hand them *RuneWarriors* and say, 'Why don't you try this and see if you're interested.'" With that advice, Curtis snapped her fingers. "Like that! There are myriad things that occur in a library that can be great, great support that a teacher isn't going to have time for. The teacher often has 30 students. In California right now they're raising the number. Don't even start," she said, bringing up Governor Arnold Schwarzenegger. "I mean he's my friend and he's having to cut, but I don't understand how a public official cuts education. I know you have to cut somewhere. Nobody wants to pay taxes.

By the way, nobody wants to pay for anything! It's crazy! And I'm in the high tax bracket. I'm paying! And I'll keep paying!" she exclaimed.

"You know, George Clooney had a great suggestion for the Screen Actors Guild. He said that for every million dollars you earn you should pay a certain amount in taxes. If every person who earns more than a million dollars has to pay that amount for every million dollars they earn . . . He came up with a great solution. Nobody wants to pay, and people have to pay for this, but it's not going to happen. What's going to happen is in 20 years we're going to be not 25th, we're going 35th on the list, and one of these years we're going to be at the bottom. And little countries like Finland are going to be above us. And someone's finally going to go, 'Because nobody wanted to pay for it.'"

"How are actors like librarians?" I asked.

"Because you're required to know a lot about everything. Actors are supposed to be able to pretend to be anything. I might need to pretend to be a brain surgeon yesterday and today I might

READ MORE

WRITTEN BY JAMIE LEE CURTIS

- *Big Words for Little People*
- *I'm Gonna Like Me: Letting Off a Little Self-Esteem*
- *It's Hard to Be Five: Learning How to Work My Control Panel*
- *My Mommy Hung the Moon: A Love Story*
- *Tell Me Again about the Night I Was Born*
- *Today I Feel Silly, and Other Moods That Make My Day*
- *When I Was Little: A Four-Year-Old's Memoir of Her Youth*
- *Where Do Balloons Go? An Uplifting Mystery*

need to pretend to be part of a beauty conglomerate and tomorrow I might need to pretend to be a schoolteacher. Every day you're an actor you're pretending to be something else but you need to have some knowledge base to pull from and librarians have a multidisciplinary knowledge. They know everything from science to math to history to English to poetry to music. They have a breadth of knowledge and they need to be able to have access to that so they can help point you in whatever direction you need to go. And an actor just honestly needs to have that same breadth of knowledge.

"The best acting teacher—the only acting teacher I ever went to—was a guy named Allan Rich. He was a character actor for years, and then later he became an acting coach, and I remember again feeling weird that I could just do this without ever going to class. And a lot of people were like, 'Who do you study with?' Well I don't study with anyone. 'You don't study with anyone? How dare you think you're an actor if you don't study with anyone?'

"So I had heard about this guy and I called him, and I remember going over to his house. And I'm not scared if you ask me to do any work, anywhere, any movie, anything, and you said 'Here read this.' I'd be like 'Done, let's go!' Whatever it is, but with him I was sitting there and I felt like I was being watched and judged by him and we did some scene from some play or some movie and I remember sitting on his couch and I finished and he said, 'Well, here's what I need to tell you. It's obvious that you know how to act like other people, pretend to be other people; that's not a problem for you. I don't think you should take acting lessons, you should just study the world. And travel and read and listen to music and have more choices to pull from.' And that's the same thing as a librarian in a way. You're not a teacher of one thing; you're a teacher of everything. And so you have to have some openness to everything. And that's a big difference. One day you might be asked about astronomy and then the next day you might be asked about rap music. And you need to have some facility to reach all of those things."

Asked what was the strangest or funniest experience she ever had in a library, Curtis reflected on her upbringing as the child of famous movie stars Janet Leigh and Tony Curtis.

"You know, I haven't spent real time in a library in quite a long time. Meaning I've been there with children, I've been there with my own children. I love the fact that at our local library, in the children's department, you could take out 20 books at a time. We used to have our big library bag and I loved that. You know what? Honestly my funny memories of that don't exist. My memories, if anything, were more restrictive; that feeling was not a good feeling for me as a child. A lot has changed, and I think that the rigidity that the movies and the media have perpetrated about librarians has changed. Now you can rent movies at libraries, you can rent books on tape, you can be on the internet, you can go to a game night. This is a community center. This is a place for all the people. And I think the more you make it accessible to all the people emotionally, not just from a technological standpoint, I think you'll bring people in."

Following her American Library Association experience in Anaheim, Jamie Lee Curtis served as honorary chair of National Library Week in 2009 and appeared in a print public service announcement under the theme "Worlds connect @ your library." ★

AL GORE

former vice president of the United States, author, environmental activist

13

THE PLANET IN THE BALANCE

"We are still in the early stages of this digital revolution."

Nobel Peace Prize and Oscar winner, former vice president, and, in his own words, the man who "used to be the next president of the United States," Al Gore delivered the Arthur Curley Memorial Lecture January 16 at the American Library Association's 2009 Midwinter Meeting in Boston. His message: The environmental threat facing the planet as a result of carbon-based fuel consumption makes all other efforts to improve the quality of human life seem futile—unless the global climate crisis is addressed, and soon.

Some 3,000 librarians filled the lecture hall to listen as he walked them through his new book, *Our Choice: A Plan to Solve the Climate Crisis*. I had an appointment to sit down and talk with Gore before the program.

An earthquake in Haiti was the news of the day, and I started the interview by noting that I had received an e-mail

Photo by Curtis Compton for the American Library Association.

from him that morning asking for contributions to disaster relief efforts.

"It's an unimaginable tragedy," Gore said. "And all of us, as Americans, all of us as human beings, are deeply touched by this tragedy and want to reach out and help those who are suffering and in distress. One of the secrets of the human condition is that suffering binds us together. And when we encounter a tragedy of this magnitude, we are left almost speechless. But we cannot fail to act. And the outpouring thus far has been heartening but much more help is needed urgently."

Gore was on a book tour for *Our Choice*, so I asked him to summarize the central message of his speaking tour.

"The climate crisis is the most serious threat that human civilization has ever confronted. It is unique in having the potential for ending human civilization as we know it, but it is not a crisis that we cannot solve. We have all the tools we need to solve three or four climate crises. We only need to solve one.

"But the missing ingredient is political will. Political will is a renewable resource; and, thus, our first challenge in solving the climate crisis is to renew our will to act urgently, boldly and effectively. *Our Choice* contains the solutions that, taken together, will actually solve the climate crisis."

"Do we have the collective will to do that?" I asked.

"We have not yet demonstrated it. But we have risen to meet seemingly impossible challenges in the past. And I have no doubt that if we choose to act, we will find sufficient reserves of will and determination to succeed. This crisis has been resistant to solution, in part because it challenges the way we think about mortal threats.

"We are predisposed, as human beings, because of our evolutionary heritage, to react most readily to the kinds of threats that our ancient ancestors survived over the millennia. But when a threat is global in nature, and when the distance between causes and consequences stretches out longer than we are used to thinking, it requires us to use our reasoning capacity and to share with one another the depth of understanding necessary to solve this crisis. We have demonstrated that capacity in the past. And there is no doubt we have it, but we must overcome the obstacles that are in our path.

"There are entrenched economic and political interests that see the solutions as a threat to their short-term profits and success. Our market system, while the best way of organizing economic activity, contains flaws that have made it difficult to use constructively in facing, in resolving this crisis, principally because we do not currently put any price on the pollution that is causing this crisis. As in times past, polluters fight against any effort to hold them accountable for the consequences of their pollution, and the general public is often less passionate than the narrow special interests that pay very close attention to anything that especially affects them.

"So we have to overcome these obstacles in our way of thinking and in the organization of our politics and economic activities. But once we overcome these obstacles, we will find that the technology and the other solutions are readily available to us."

Librarians are in the business of free and open access to information, I pointed out, and they are also in the business of guiding people to accurate and authoritative information. But when it comes to global warming, there are a lot of naysayers. What do we say to them?

READ MORE

Recommended by AL GORE

- ★ The books of Marshall McLuhan and Mark Twain

"Libraries were born, of course, in the age of print. The printing press, beginning in the middle of the 15th century, radically reorganized the information ecosystem within which human civilization addresses challenges. By opening up access to information to publics rather than constricting it to elites, as was the case with the monastic scriptorium and the information system of the Middle Ages—which lasted from the fall of Rome through the Renaissance and then the Enlightenment—the printing press democratized information and created a meritocracy of ideas that allowed the illiterate masses to judge for themselves what was more likely than not to be true. As access to information was refeudalized in the era of broadcasting, the ability of elites to shape the information that had the most impact on publics tempted them to undermine the rule of reason by a variety of techniques, including, shamefully, the intentional dissemination of information known to be inaccurate in order to intentionally confuse people into believing that controversies existed in science where, really, a very firm consensus had been developed.

"These techniques were most famously used by the tobacco companies to undermine the medical consensus linking the smoking of cigarettes to diseases of the lung and heart and arteries. And some of the same practitioners of those techniques carried them to the large carbon polluters, who have spent

The printing press democratized information and created a meritocracy of ideas that allowed the illiterate masses to judge for themselves what was more likely than not to be true. —AL GORE

approximately a billion dollars per year to create the false impression that there is massive disagreement in the scientific community about the climate crisis. In reality, there is as strong a consensus as you will ever find in science. And the great challenge now is to reject the false information and construct policies on the basis of what is known to be true."

More than a decade ago, *American Libraries* magazine ran a picture of Gore and President Clinton wiring a cable at a high school in California. But since then, wireless access and cell phones and various kinds of social media have just bloomed in our culture. I asked him what he thought librarians and educators need to do to help young people use them in a positive way.

"The internet is destined to have an even larger impact on civilization than did the printing press," he replied. "But we are still in the early stages of this digital revolution. Marshall McLuhan wrote many decades ago that when one is caught in a whirlpool, the impulse to swim against the current is often the wrong response. By swimming with the current, one can emerge from the gyre and live to see a new day. The fundamental characteristics of the internet are surprisingly similar to those of the printing press in that the barriers to access for individuals are extremely low. And it brings with it the potential to once again democratize access to information and re-create a meritocracy of ideas.

"Libraries face a daunting but exciting challenge in adapting to this new technology, swimming with the current, and making the best of its positive characteristics even as they keep a weather eye for the negative characteristics, which are always present in any information medium."

A decade or more ago, there was a lot of concern being expressed about protecting children online, protecting them from predators and pornography, I noted, and asked how well he thought we were doing, especially in view of the blossoming of social media.

"The good news is that many powerful digital tools have been integrated into the technologies of the internet that enable adults to protect children if they are diligent in doing so. The less good news is that the emergent culture of the internet has eroded that diligence and has created some genuine threats to young children who are not beneficiaries of the kind of adult care and diligence that is even more important when the kinds of images and information that young children are not prepared to process are so ubiquitously available if they do not receive the love and attention of their parents, teachers, and librarians."

In *Our Choice* Gore wrote that "the volume of information flowing between machines now far exceeds the flow of information between human beings." I asked him what we were to make of that.

"There are now one billion transistors for every human being on earth," he observed. "The distribution of intelligent information-processing devices throughout the built environment, throughout our civilization, is leading to yet another radical transformation of the information ecosystem. And as is almost always the case with powerful new technologies, we face the threats that both Prometheus and Faust in different ways confronted. And those two legends are different and important particulars; the message of each is that when we gain new power, we have to pay adequate attention to the ethical context within which it is used and take care to accelerate the emergence of sufficient wisdom to gain the benefits without falling prey to the unintended, harmful consequences."

I asked Gore what he recalled about librarians and teachers in his life and if they helped him develop good learning habits, especially when it comes to controversial topics. I asked if he had any particular memories of special people or libraries that he used.

"The most salient memories are emotional memories, feeling that the library was like a candy store just filled with joy and ex-

The library was like a candy store just filled with joy and excitement, and the presence of guides who could point you toward the good stuff was essential. — AL GORE

citement, and the presence of guides who could point you toward the good stuff was essential," he said.

I asked what he personally valued about libraries. Again, he invoked perspectives derived from a knowledge of history.

"One of the greatest impacts of the printing press, again, was the democratization of knowledge and the emergence of an ability to use ideas and information as a source of new power in the hands of the average person to reclaim control of his or her destiny. And libraries became the fortresses of knowledge, accessible to all, regardless of wealth, power, family connections or any other sources of power in the world that preceded the Enlightenment. Like all new eras, the Enlightenment also brought risks but on balance was the greatest advance for human civilization that we've ever experienced, and the library as an institution was both the symbol and the most powerful institution in spreading access to that knowledge."

"Do you have a sense of the library as a sort of lifelong learning experience, where you have preschool story hours in your public library and then you have the school library and then you go to the university library and then back to the public?" I asked.

"Yes, I do," Gore said. "But like many, I now am able to supplement the library as we used to know it with a library that has no walls. And librarians have been very energetic and imaginative in taking advantage of these new digital capabilities that extend their reach and allow them to connect with many more people."

I asked Gore to talk about the Library of Congress having so much of its collection available digitally and online to the American public, permitting the kind of access people have never had before.

"Indeed," he said. "And during my service in the House and Senate and White House, I was an advocate for the digitization of libraries and the creation of opportunities for people to connect to libraries digitally. In the early days of my advocacy of what I call the information superhighway, I used one seminal image over and over again when I asked audiences to imagine a young girl in Carthage, Tennessee, population 2,000, my hometown, coming home after school and plugging into the Library of Congress and perusing its vast knowledge at her own speed and pace and navigating by her own curiosity and learning according to her own desires."

In preparing to talk with Gore, I had gone to snopes.com to see if the website was debunking the legend that Gore once

READ MORE

Written by Al Gore

- ★ *The Assault on Reason*
- ★ *Earth in the Balance: Ecology and the Human Spirit*
- ★ *Our Choice: A Plan to Solve the Climate Crisis*
- ★ *An Inconvenient Truth: The Planetary Emergency of Global Warming and What We Can Do about It*

claimed to have invented the internet. That finally got a laugh out of him, and he said he did not know about snopes.com. I told him that the site did contain a piece explaining that he had never said that. I asked him to comment on that kind of misinformation and how it can just stick.

"Well, I'm far from the only one who's experienced that phenomenon," he said, grinning and more or less dismissing the rumor. "Mark Twain wrote in the 19th century that a lie, it runs around the world before the truth gets its boots on. So it's not uncommon, really."

I mentioned that the image people have of Gore as stiff and aristocratic seems to have changed over the years, perhaps because he has appeared on *Saturday Night Live* and other television shows and joked about himself. "Do you think that it has really changed people's openness to you and your message?" I asked.

Gore thought about his answer for a moment and said, "I've been very fortunate in my life. And following the 2000 election, I was fortunate to find other ways to serve and to be of use and to try my best to bring a positive change to the world. And I'm still trying." ★

OPRAH WINFREY

television talk show host, media mogul

14

READING FOR LIFE

"I don't believe in failure."

Okay, so this chapter is a stretch because I have never interviewed Oprah Winfrey; I have never even met her. But when you talk about reading with the stars, who among them has had more of an impact on American reading habits than this extraordinary television talk show host?

The ways Oprah Winfrey has supported the programs and mission of American libraries are legion.

Librarians have been connected to Oprah's Book Club since its inception in 1996. Publishers of the chosen titles have sent approximately 10,000 copies of each Oprah-selected book to some 3,560 public and high school libraries and other institutional members of the American Library Association. Each library receives up to five copies, depending on its size. The publishers of Oprah's Book Club selections have distributed more than 600,000 free books to member libraries. Winfrey has made this distribution a central part of her book club, providing libraries across the country with new ways to increase the circulation of good books.

Oprah visits the Chris Hani Independence School in South Africa in 2003.
Photo by Benny Gool, courtesy of Harpo, Inc.

Oprah's Book Club spawned new interest in reading discussion groups and rocketed every selection to the top of best-seller lists. With 40 million viewers per week, *The Oprah Winfrey Show* boosted sales for each title from thousands to hundreds of thousands or, in many cases, millions.

From a childhood of abuse in a home with no electricity or running water, Winfrey became one of the most influential people in history as host of a television show that reached not only 40 million Americans every week but millions more in 148 countries. By age 49 she was a self-made billionaire, ruling a vast entertainment and communications empire and symbolizing what an ambitious individual could achieve in America. "I don't believe in failure," she has been quoted as saying.

"Books were my path to personal freedom," Winfrey has also said. "I learned to read at age 3 and soon discovered there was a whole world to conquer that went beyond our farm in Mississippi." She credits her father with understanding the value of education: "Because of his respect for education and my stepmother's respect for education, every single week of my life that I lived with them I had to read library books and that was the beginning of the book club. Who knew? But I was reading books and had to do book reports in my own house. Now at 9 years old, nobody wants to have to do book reports in addition to what the school is asking you to do, but my father's insistence that education was the open door to freedom is what allows me to stand here today a free woman."

Noting on her television show in August of 2000 that *Good Housekeeping* had reported that 77% of elementary teachers say that children return to school reading below or at the same level because they just have been out of practice, Winfrey boosted summer reading, saying that too many kids "really are taking the summer off." She suggested that to encourage a young reader, "you have to insist on 15 to 30 minutes every day to read. You

Getting my library card was like citizenship; it was like American citizenship. — OPRAH WINFREY

just do." Winfrey credited her stepmother with having done so. "We would go to the library and would draw books every two weeks. I would take out five books, and I would have a little reading time every day. That's what encouraged me to become a great reader. Who knew I was going to grow up to have my own book club? But you have to do that with your children, and your children need to see you reading."

Winfrey said that it is not enough to simply tell children to read but never have books in the house. "You make a field trip of a day to the library, and make a big deal out of getting your own library card," she advised. "And make sure you have books available at home to read. Have your child read aloud so that you can gauge their progress. That's another good thing to do. And try to get them hooked on a favorite author or a series, like when I was a girl it was *Strawberry Girl* by Lois Lenski and that whole series by Lois Lenski."

In 2008, the Association for Library Service to Children collaborated with *The Oprah Winfrey Show* to include "Kids' Reading List" on www.oprah.com, divided into five age groups, from infant to age 12 and up. Each group contained an annotated bibliography of librarian-recommended reading. The website also provided a list of ways to make reading fun for kids and other helpful tips for parents.

"By teaming up with Oprah's Book Club, we're able to connect with a wide range of people we may not have reached otherwise. Whether children come into our library or are given a book from our recommended reading list, we are helping our youngest and most important patrons," said librarian Pat Scales of "Kids' Reading List."

In 1997, at its Annual Conference in San Francisco, the American Library Association bestowed its highest award on Winfrey, Honorary Membership for life. The honoree was unable to accept the award in person because she was in production with her film *Beloved*, but she sent a statement of gratitude that was read during the opening session. "I am delighted that the American Library Association wishes to bestow an Honorary Membership upon me," Winfrey said. Wishing the association "continued success," she added, "Know that I appreciate you thinking of me."

The award citation reads: "Oprah Winfrey, through her Book Club, has done more to revitalize and promote the importance of reading among American citizens than any other public figure in recent times. Through libraries, she has helped make books available free of charge to many who might not have been able to purchase their own copies. She has refocused attention on the important role of the library in the community."

Books allowed me to see a world beyond the front porch of my grandmother's shotgun house and gave me the power to see possibilities beyond what was allowed at the time; beyond economic and social realities; beyond classrooms with no books and unqualified teachers; beyond false beliefs and prejudice that veiled the minds of so many men and women of the time.

— OPRAH WINFREY

In 2004 Winfrey accepted the United Nations Association of the United States of America Global Humanitarian Award, saying: "As a young girl in Mississippi, I had big dreams at a time when being a Negro child you weren't supposed to dream big. I dreamed anyway. Books did that for me. Books allowed me to see a world beyond the front porch of my grandmother's shotgun house and gave me the power to see possibilities beyond what was allowed at the time; beyond economic and social realities; beyond classrooms with no books and unqualified teachers; beyond false beliefs and prejudice that veiled the minds of so many men and women of the time. For me, those dreams started when I heard the stories of my rich heritage. When I read about Sojourner Truth and Harriet Tubman and Mary McLeod Bethune and Frederick Douglass. I knew that there was possibility for me."

Winfrey has also been a champion of intellectual freedom and journalist integrity.

In 2008, when the superintendent of schools in Loudoun County, Virginia, decided to remove *And Tango Makes Three,* an award-winning children's book by Peter Parnell and Justin Richardson about two male penguins hatching and parenting a baby chick, Winfrey criticized the removal on her show.

In 2006, Winfrey's on-air scolding of author James Frey for falsifying sections of his book *A Million Little Pieces* made television history, forcing him to admit that portions of his Oprah's Book Club selection, a wrenching memoir about addiction, were complete fiction. Scheduled to be interviewed onstage at the 2008 American Library Association's conference in Anaheim, Frey had to cancel at the last minute, but the whole controversy had created a call to action for the publishing industry.

The American Library Association received an Oprah's Angel Network Book Club Award for $50,000 to support the Young Adult Library Services Association's Great Stories Club, a national reading and discussion program. The award was announced on the October 26, 2005, episode of *The Oprah Winfrey Show*. Two years later, Oprah's Angel Network awarded $300,000 to the Great Stories Club. The new funding allowed the program to continue for three more years, reaching 700 libraries and distributing more than 20,000 new books to teens.

"We're pleased to provide additional funding to the ALA Great Stories Club," Caren Yanis, then executive director of Oprah's Angel Network, said at the time. "We're inspired that this program not only provides meaningful books to at-risk and underserved youth, but also that it addresses the importance of creating opportunities for these young people to share and discuss their own stories with their peers. As a result of this program, we look forward to seeing many more young people positively impacted by their involvement with reading and libraries."

Of the Great Stories Club, then American Library Association president Loriene Roy said, "Many teens owned or read a book from cover to cover for the first time because of this program, which created new community partnerships and provided service to an overlooked, under-resourced group of young readers."

On January 2, 2007, celebrities lined up in the small town of Henley-on-Klip, in the Gauteng province of South Africa, to back Winfrey as she opened her new $40 million Leadership Academy for Girls. Designed to raise girls from poverty to positions of leadership, the academy is equipped with a state-of-the-art library. Built on a 52-acre campus, the 28-building complex also includes computer and science labs, a theater, and a wellness center.

Nelson Mandela, whom Winfrey credited with inspiring her to build the school, attended the opening ceremony. The anti-apartheid leader who became South Africa's first democratically elected president in 1994 told Winfrey, "This is not a distant donation but a project that clearly lies close to your heart." The school enabled poor children, grades 7 through 12, from all over

South Africa, to attain an education that would otherwise be impossible.

"These girls deserve to be surrounded by beauty, and beauty does inspire," Winfrey told *Newsweek*. "I wanted this to be a place of honor for them because these girls have never been treated with kindness. They've never been told they are pretty or have wonderful dimples. I wanted to hear those things as a child."

Other celebrities in attendance included Sidney Poitier, Tina Turner, Mariah Carey, Mary J. Blige, Chris Rock, and Spike Lee. The guests were asked to bring a personally inscribed book for the library. Donations ranged from self-help manuals and literary classics to titles in the Harry Potter series. Winfrey said she brought the celebrity entourage because "these people have the power to do things; they have voices which can be heard in the United States and across the world."

"We asked each of you to bring your favorite book because, as you all know, I love books," Winfrey told the celebrities. "I believe books are the foundation for learning, and we wanted all of our guests to help build our library."

The year before, Winfrey had handpicked the first two classes of 7th- and 8th-grade students who were to attend the Leadership Academy. To qualify, the girls had to come from households with a monthly income of not more than 5,000 rand (about $787) and had to have exhibited academic talent and leadership ability in their communities.

READ MORE

Recommended by OPRAH WINFREY

- A complete list of Oprah's Book Club selections and the Kids' Reading Lists are available at oprah.com

"When you educate a woman, you set her free," Winfrey has said. "Had I not had books and education in Mississippi, I would have believed that's all there was."

In 1987, years before she started her Book Club but already the star of the number one talk show on television, Winfrey posed for an American Library Association Celebrity READ poster, which also made the November cover of *American Libraries*. Winfrey posed for the photograph on a sunny day in Chicago's Grant Park with her "all-time favorite book," *Their Eyes Were Watching God,* by Zora Neale Hurston. She said at the time that she read five books a week to prepare for her show, and her "passion" was browsing in bookstores, "looking for the right book, the one you can't put down."

Winfrey's film company, Harpo Films, has produced projects based on classic and contemporary literature—just another way she has brought great works to the attention of a viewing audience, which often then goes back to read the book, so it's full circle. Telefilms under the "Oprah Winfrey Presents" banner have included the award-winning *Tuesdays with Morrie*, based on the best-selling novel by Mitch Albom and starring Academy Award winner Jack Lemmon and Emmy Award winner Hank Azaria; and *Their Eyes Were Watching God,* based on the Zora Neale Hurston novel and starring Academy Award winner Halle Berry. Plus Harpo Films produced *Beloved,* a Touchstone Pictures feature film based on the Pulitzer Prize–winning novel by Toni Morrison, which co-starred Winfrey and Danny Glover and was directed by Jonathan Demme.

"When I was a kid and the other kids were home watching *Leave It to Beaver,*" Winfrey has said, "my father and stepmother were marching me off to the library." She put it this way: "Getting my library card was like citizenship; it was like American citizenship." ★